CW00385503

Marketing Strategy

for effective fundraising

Peter Maple

DIRECTORY OF SOCIAL CHANGE

Published by the Directory of Social Change (registered Charity no. 80051)

Head office: 24 Stephenson Way, London NW1 2DP

Northern office: Federation House, Hope Street, Liverpool L1 9BW
Tel: 08450 77 77 07

Visit www.dsc.org.uk to find out more about our books, subscription funding websites and training events. You can also sign up for e-newsletters so that you're always the first to hear about what's new.

The publisher welcomes suggestions and comments that will help to inform and improve future versions of this and all of our titles. Please give us your feedback by emailing publications@dsc.org.uk.

It should be understood that this publication is intended for guidance only and is not a substitute for professional or legal advice. No responsibility for loss occasioned as a result of any person acting or refraining from acting can be accepted by the authors or publisher.

First published 2003
Second edition 2013

ISBN 978 1 906294 59 5

British Library Cataloguing in Publication Data
A catalogue record for this book is available from the British Library

Cover design by Kate Bass
Original text design by Eugenie Dodd Typographics
Typeset by Marlinzo Services, Frome
Printed and bound by Page Bros, Norwich

MIX
Paper from
responsible sources
FSC
www.fsc.org
FSC® C023114

I would like to dedicate this edition to two remarkable men who, in very different ways, changed the face of fundraising. They both, with their unique styles, had a profound effect upon me when I entered the voluntary sector in 1990 and, I believe, made me a far better and more thoughtful fundraiser as a result. Luke FitzHerbert and Redmond Mullin left their mark on the sector and I pay tribute to their contributions.

Contents

The Fundraising Series

The trouble with change is that it never stands still! And that is no less true for fundraising than any other professional discipline. The economy, political landscape and the ways people exchange information and communicate with each other all impact on the way in which charities ask for, and raise money. That is what makes fundraising such a challenging and dynamic profession. I am not sure I will be popular for comparing fundraising to dabbling in stock market futures, but successful fundraisers are often those who can predict and be responsive to social change and be able to adapt their fundraising strategies accordingly – to be effective it is vital to stay ahead of the game.

The Directory of Social Change's Fundraising Series seeks to address the full range of fundraising activity and techniques in one series. Each successive volume seeks to address one key element in the spectrum of fundraising techniques. As fundraising techniques evolve and develop, new titles in the series are added to and old ones revised.

The titles are intended as texts that encourage and debate fundraising within a professional framework – written and used by academics and practitioners alike. Each title seeks to explore a fundraising activity within its historical, ethical and theoretical context, relate it to current fundraising practice and guide future strategy.

We thank all those who have contributed and continue to contribute to the most comprehensive fundraising series available today.

Debra Allcock Tyler
Chief Executive, Directory of Social Change

About the Directory of Social Change

DSC has a vision of an independent voluntary sector at the heart of social change. The activities of independent charities, voluntary organisations and community groups are fundamental to achieve social change. We exist to help these organisations and the people who support them to achieve their goals.

We do this by:

• providing practical tools that organisations and activists need, including online and printed publications, training courses, and conferences on a huge range of topics;

• acting as a 'concerned citizen' in public policy debates, often on behalf of smaller charities, voluntary organisations and community groups;

• leading campaigns and stimulating debate on key policy issues that affect those groups;

• carrying out research and providing information to influence policymakers.

DSC is the leading provider of information and training for the voluntary sector and publishes an extensive range of guides and handbooks covering subjects such as fundraising, management, communication, finance and law. We have a range of subscription-based websites containing a wealth of information on funding from trusts, companies and government sources. We run more than 300 training courses each year, including bespoke in-house training provided at the client's location. DSC conferences, many of which run on an annual basis, include the Charity Management Conference, the Charity Accountants' Conference and the Charity Law Conference. DSC's major annual event is Charityfair, which provides low-cost training on a wide variety of subjects.

For details of all our activities, and to order publications and book courses, go to www.dsc.org.uk, call 08450 777707 or email publications@dsc.org.uk

About the author

Peter Maple is Course Director at London South Bank University, developing and delivering fundraising and strategic marketing for its highly successful MSc Management in Civil Society programme. He supervises research concerning charity fundraising and is a coach, mentor and strategic consultant. He is also undertaking a PhD examining the nature of philanthropy.

He is the author of a number of successful published papers and books. Unique among fundraising academics, Peter has been a successful fundraising practitioner and director of fundraising for more than 20 years. Senior posts held at major charities include the YMCA, Arthritis Care, Leonard Cheshire Disability, The Brooke Hospital for Animals and Crisis UK. He is both an effective practitioner and respected academic.

Acknowledgements

Firstly I would like to acknowledge what has, for me, been most important of all in writing this second edition, and that is the wholehearted support of my partner Norma who is not only a consummate psychotherapist but who gave me vital reality checks on the text at key moments. Her proof reading of six drafts and helpful (though sometimes resented) feedback ensured that the text is, I believe, very accessible.

Furthermore, without the insights of the many named and anonymous contributors whom I interviewed this would be a very dry theoretical tome. To everyone, but especially my colleagues, Alex Murdock, Nigel Scott and Bruce Lloyd at London South Bank University, who have helped and encouraged me in the production of this new edition and ensured that it is well-grounded, thank you.

Those who kindly provided insights for either this edition or the first edition, and some for both, include Marion Allford, Steve Andrews, Simon Armson, Mark Astarita, Judy Beard, Margaret Bennett, Simon Burne, Simon Collings, Tony Cram, Sue Daniels, Ceri Edwards, Tony Elischer, Peter Flory, Richard Gutch, Verity Haines, Christine Holland, Andrew Hope, Jeremy Hughes, Howard Lake, Richard Lee, Bruce Lloyd, Tony Manwaring, Redmond Mullin, Kate Nash, Phil Nunn, Giles Pegram, Cathy Pharoah, Stephen Pidgeon, Jeremy Prescot, Judith Rich, Kim Roberts, David Saint, Joe Saxton, George Smith, Peter Sweatman, David Tootill, Ian Ventham, Peter Vickery-Smith, Mike Wade, and Jackie White.

I would also like to thank the following organisations for allowing me to reproduce text, images, charts, advertisements and for providing information for case studies: Amnesty International Aotearoa New Zealand, Arthritis Care, Barnardo's, British Diabetic Association, British Red Cross, The Brooke (Brooke Hospital for Animals), Cancer Research UK, Cards for Good Causes, Colenso BBDO, Crisis UK, Crossbow Research, Kilmartin Baker, Leonard Cheshire Disability, Macmillan Cancer Support, NDCS, NSPCC, Oxfam, Remember A Charity, RNLI, SouthBank Mosaics, and, lastly, my band, The Touch.

Finally a mention for all my postgraduate fundraising students at London South Bank University, past and present (and, I hope, future). They, more than most, inspire me to go on researching philanthropy and teaching fundraising. They listen attentively and challenge anything that is not evidenced well. Their shared experiences are invaluable in keeping me up to date, with my nose on the ball, and I thank them for allowing me to continue mixing my metaphors!

Foreword

It was particularly gratifying to be asked to write the foreword to this text. Peter Maple's text is just one of three books currently addressing what is an increasingly significant topic and its progression to a second edition is timely. We live in an age when the UK government is increasingly extolling the virtues of the 'Big Society' as a way of tackling society's ills, yet seems unwilling to make the necessary investment of resources that would equip the sector to deliver the desired impact. Demands on the sector are rising as a consequence and organisations are expected to generate their own resources to make this provision a reality. It is now more important than ever, therefore, that nonprofits learn how to understand the needs of their stakeholders, design programmes and services to meet the needs of these audiences and deliver them in a way that delivers genuine value for society.

Maple's text offers genuine insight into how this might best be accomplished. The author draws on learning taken from both the commercial and nonprofit domains to demonstrate how our nonprofit community can satisfactorily achieve these goals. The author has a wealth of practical experience gained at a senior level that allows him to paint a rich picture of how the tools and techniques of marketing can be used to good effect.

It is interesting to note that it has now been more than 40 years since Kotler and Levy first dared to suggest that marketing tools and ideas might have relevance outside of the business domain. It seems hard to believe now that their ideas were hotly contested at the time and it is now widely acknowledged that nonprofits can benefit at least as much from the practice of marketing as their commercial counterparts. They too, need to understand critical concepts such as segmentation, targeting and positioning, the key elements of a marketing mix and the latest thinking in consumer and donor behaviour that can inform the design of communications.

The past 30 years have seen a succession of important milestones in the creation of the new field of nonprofit marketing, including the publication of three dedicated academic journals, the appearance of numerous special interest groups in marketing professional bodies around the world and the creation of master's degrees specifically focused on individuals wishing to practice in this context. While nonprofit marketing will always be firmly grounded in practice it is increasingly recognised as an important avenue for academic study and research in its own right. Such scholarly thinking and research is now aiding a wide variety of organisations, from soup kitchens to hospitals, to do a better job of both promoting their services to clients and generating the income necessary to sustain the services they provide.

Maple's text provides a window on this thinking and is one of the few that will be of interest to both an academic and a professional audience. The text that follows is written to offer practical value to those working in the field, but also to support those studying the topic of nonprofit marketing at a college or University. Whatever your primary purpose, you will find value in this text and I commend it to you.

Adrian Sargeant
Robert F. Hartsook Professor of Fundraising, Indiana University

Preface

The first edition of *Marketing Strategy for Effective Fundraising* was very well received by practitioners and academics alike when it was published by the Directory of Social Change in 2003. It filled an important gap between the well-grounded 'how to' guides and the more academically inclined textbooks on marketing and fundraising management.

This second edition has been extensively updated with new case studies, and the latest research and practitioner thinking. Included for the first time are some original ideas about important concepts, including that of developing the right case for support. The book aims to answer the three questions that anyone thinking about giving will ask. *What* do you do? Why do *you* do it? And, most importantly, why should *I* support you?

My hope, therefore, is that this new edition will appeal even more to fundraisers and marketeers who are seeking to become better practitioners, managers and directors. And, finally, since good marketing depends so much on useful feedback, I encourage any readers' comments or advice on the text.

CHAPTER ONE

Why charities need marketing and marketing needs charities

Marketing is philosophically and practically well suited to the voluntary and public sectors.
Ian Bruce

There's always a better deal to be had.
Chester Karass

This chapter examines the context in which civil society organisations (CSOs) operate today, contrasting for-profit and not-for-profit marketing practices and considering the benefits of each sector learning from the other. Importantly, this chapter aims to show that while charities have a great need to adopt effective integrated commercial marketing practices, for-profit organisations ignore the best of what social marketing offers at their peril.

Perspectives

The advent of active fundraising in the UK can be dated back at least to the eleventh century. Marketing is a rather younger concept for both commercial and voluntary organisations but its importance to fundraising in the not-for-profit sector, including all but the smallest of charities, has perhaps never been as great.

There is no single reason for this. Marketing has not been imposed out of the blue on an unsuspecting industry, but as the not-for-profit sector has developed it has become aware of the benefits that a marketing strategy, plans and initiatives can bring in meeting the challenges faced by CSOs today.

While the language of marketing may not always come easily to many people operating in the sector, the strategy and practices that it imposes are crucial to the success of CSOs. If the word 'brand' grates then, as Joe Saxton (2002) who is the 'driver of ideas' for nfpSynergy suggests, 'each time you read the word "brand" mentally replace it with the word "image" or "reputation"'. This advice, if followed, could help many trustees and volunteers begin to understand just how much value is locked-up within the name and reputation of a well-known national organisation.

1

Chapter 4 will look in depth at brand issues, particularly as they relate to CSOs.

Some definitions

As figure 1.1 shows, public, private and not-for-profit sectors can be thought of in a number of ways and there is considerable overlap in their spheres of operation. Community interest companies (CICs) and social enterprises can be considered as hybrids between private and public sectors, or not-for-profit and private sectors; in this way, they can be thought of as the overlapping area in the middle. This area is capable of very significant growth and Chapter 7 offers further comment on this subject (see page 110).

FIGURE 1.1 INTERLOCKING CIRCLES OF PUBLIC, PRIVATE AND NOT-FOR-PROFIT ORGANISATIONAL ACTIVITY

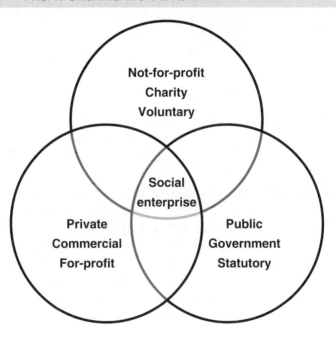

Marketing

Classic definitions of marketing range from 'creating value by fulfilling customer needs' to 'the management process responsible for identifying, anticipating and satisfying customer requirements profitably' (CIM 2009a). In essence, most definitions have the common elements of delivering satisfaction and value while maintaining a sustainable business.

Charities might argue that their particular role – to change the world – is inimical to this business ethos. However, given that every established charity recognises that the problems it seeks to address are, by definition, intractable, complex and long-term, there is an equal argument in favour of considering how good commercial practices might be successfully applied to the task. Philip Kotler's definition, developed in the 1970s and aimed principally at service providers, still fits the bill rather well for CSOs. He said: 'Marketing is the analysis, planning, implementation and control of carefully formulated programs designed to bring about voluntary exchanges of values with target markets for the purpose of achieving organizational objectives' (Kotler 1975). Incidentally the Merriam-Webster (2012) online dictionary states that a 'marketeer' is 'a specialist in promoting or selling a product or service' (first mentioned in 1832) and a 'marketer' is 'one that promotes or sells a product or service' (first mentioned in 1787). The author's preference is for the later, more specialist term 'marketeer' and so this is used throughout the book.

Direct marketing and direct mail

Direct marketing is often confused with direct mail, but direct mail is just one medium that is used in direct marketing. It also includes the use of the telephone, the Internet and now, interestingly, a return to face-to-face dialogue in the form of street, workplace and house-to-house canvassing (see also 'Direct mail', page 98).

Social marketing

Nearly twenty years on and Kotler (1994) defines social marketing as:

> The societal marketing concept holds that the organization's task is to determine the needs, wants and interests of target markets and to deliver the desired satisfactions more effectively and efficiently than competitors in a way that preserves or enhances the consumer's and the society's well-being.

In other words, running a sustainable business while delivering a social benefit.

It is important to note that many aspects of marketing that have been developed successfully by charities are ignored by commercial organisations at their peril. A main argument of this book is that the two sectors

3

still have much to learn from one another. While commercial marketing models may not transplant successfully into CSOs, it is certain that many good marketing practices, if they are integrated and understood well by all who must contribute, will be enormously beneficial to those charities which adopt them successfully. The return to for-profit organisations will, equally, this book contends, produce strong marketing advantages.

Integrated marketing

The for-profit sector has embraced an integrated approach to marketing for decades. Indeed from global players to sole traders, the requirement to differentiate and meet customer need in competition with other providers has meant that marketing considerations permeate organisations both vertically and horizontally. That is, good marketing planning tends to work from the board right down to the newest trainees and across functions including production, distribution, administration and human resources. With this in mind, another main argument of this book is that strategic marketing needs to be fully integrated into an entire CSO's strategic management plans and operations so that it becomes part of the culture. A global service provider such as HSBC is interesting in its approach to its reputation and the case study quoted in Chapter 2 goes into more detail about this, see page 20.

Consider the competition

In the voluntary sector which, according to *The UK Civil Society Almanac*, encompasses in the UK 163,800 voluntary organisations and more than 700,000 further civil society organisations (Clark et al. 2012), competition between charities is inevitable and probably beneficial. Should a prospective giver want to support a cancer charity, they can choose Macmillan, Marie Curie, Cancer Research UK, Breakthrough, BACUP, and hundreds more national and smaller, local organisations. Even making a second-level choice to give just to a cancer-care organisation, or a charity focused on a specific cancer, leaves a large number of possible candidates for support.

If our hypothetical giver's interest is in children's charities, the choice can seem equally bewildering. The first to be formed, the Thomas Coram Foundation for Children (for abandoned babies and children) dates back to 1739 and was originally called the Foundling Hospital. It is still going strong under the working name Coram. Dr Barnardo's, National Children's Home (now Action for Children), the Children's Society and the NSPCC were all founded within a few years of each other in the nineteenth century, each from a different religious basis. Now these five organisations coexist alongside thousands of other children's charities. A similar situation exists for disability charities, medical research, animal protection, and just about any other cause a giver might wish to support.

It is perhaps natural that charities should diversify and propagate themselves. A national organisation may be founded to address a major illness, such as multiple sclerosis. It will soon experience numerous demands from those who live with, or are in the shadow of, this condition for research into a cure, for respite and care support, for self-help groups, for information on accessible lifestyles, and these demands will themselves be replicated at a local level. Only the strongest and wealthiest of organisations can effectively address such a range of demands. The most likely model is for local, specialist charities to be established, supporting, for example, self-help groups in the north east of England; and these smaller niche charities are as likely to be independent of a national organisation as they are to operate under its wider umbrella. Such a scenario has been played out time and again.

Mergers

A more recent trend, however, is for the unification of charities. These range from the merger some years ago of a number of charities for the visually impaired under the umbrella organisation Action for Blind People (itself now part of an enlarged RNIB Group), to the merger of numerous HIV and AIDS charities with the far better known Terrence Higgins Trust. This particular charity has continued to prosper in the face of declining fortunes for many AIDS support organisations and has taken on the mantles of those which would otherwise have been compelled to close due to changes in funding or need (or both). In addition, the very important combination of national charity giants Imperial Cancer Research Fund (ICRF) and Cancer Research Campaign (CRC) to produce Cancer Research UK (CRUK) was a sign of many more mergers to come. The merger of Help the Aged and Age Concern in 2008 is a further example of the trend. And Richard Gutch (2012), having assisted the formation of Disability Rights UK from the merger of three charities, has even written *The Good Merger Guide*.

Case study: The formation of Cancer Research UK

Talks about a possible merger between the two giants ICRF and CRC (both had turnovers in excess of £100 million) dated back to 1980. A merger was finally agreed and the new charity, CRUK, came into existence in July 2002. An important factor for both boards of trustees was – after much analysis of respective supporter databases – a firm belief that, overall, greater net funding for cancer research could be generated by a single merged operation. Indeed, income has continued to grow and in 2011 the charity raised almost £515 million.

Peter Vickery-Smith, then director of marketing and fundraising at CRUK, argued that cross-sector partnerships and campaigns often become confused and can lead to mismanagement. He believed that 'charities need to be brave enough to take the extra step [of considering mergers]'. His view of the ICRF and CRC merger is that it has led to increased flexibility and improved service delivery. He felt that charities must acknowledge that the increasingly saturated marketplace could pose real threats to the continuing health of the voluntary sector and that more charities should, therefore, consider merging to increase public confidence in the sector.

The landscape of the voluntary sector is made up of many thousands of similar organisations competing for funds, volunteers and service users. While overall numbers of charities remain largely static, thousands of new charities are being formed and registered each year: in 2011/12 more than 5,600 charities joined the register (Charity Commission 2012).

Even in the area of higher education mergers are not just a theoretical option to maximise growth and competitiveness but are actually happening among some of the major players. In 2002, Manchester University and UMIST announced plans to merge to become Britain's largest university with up to 28,000 full-time students. In August of the same year London Guildhall and UNL (University of North London) merged to form the London Metropolitan University with up to 25,000 students.

Perhaps most surprising of all was the proposed merger of Imperial College and University College London (UCL). UCL already faced well-publicised financial deficits and Dr Chris Towler, Imperial's then director of strategy and development, admitted that while the universities collaborate in many ways they are forced to compete for research funding (Alleyne 2002). The hope was that as a giant international player with a turnover of more than £800 million the new institution would attract more research funding than traditional competitors. However by November 2002, amidst acrimony and accusations, the proposed merger was called off (MacLeod 2002).

The huge reductions in government funding through the Higher Education Funding Council for England announced in 2010 and inevitable large increases in fee levels are certain to spark another round of merger proposals.

Consortia and collaboration

Mergers are, of course, only one avenue of cooperation and other less final solutions are open to those wishing to solve particular marketing problems. Assisi is a payroll-giving consortium originally formed by 11 animal-oriented charities to promote and develop employee support through payroll donations. Many of the collaborating partners were very small and had little public profile, and so workplace canvassing would have been unlikely to prove cost-effective for them. Assisi has been enormously successful in acting as a single point of reference for those interested in helping animals via salary deductions, so much so that it has now been constituted as a charity in its own right, with the remit to raise funds for the member charities. There are also moves to share back-office facilities, and to take advantage of group purchasing schemes in order to reduce costs and to improve effectiveness. In 2011 there were five core members – Blue Cross, World Horse Welfare, SPANA, Mayhew Animal Home and the Animal Health Trust – which benefited from around £300,000 per year raised on their behalf (Assisi 2011, 2012).

In a similar way, Four Cs, Card Aid (which is run by the Charities Advisory Trust) and Cards for Good Causes has had great success in the charity Christmas card market – a market which generates an estimated £50 million in donations for charities in the UK (GCA 2012). The following case study shows how this organisation came about.

Case study: The Cards for Good Causes collaboration (CFGC)

Founder and former chief executive of CFGC Judith Rich says, 'the initial impetus to provide better distribution for the member charities just grew and grew'. When Rich arrived in 1976 there were just 17 charities loosely cooperating as the '1959 group' over cards in one another's own charity shops. With Rich's drive, enthusiasm and determination the consortium never looked back.

Independent outlets and temporary shops in halls, churches and empty shops are secured each year. Central warehousing for participating charities' cards has been introduced and the number of guest charities which participate in selected shops in return for providing volunteers to help staff those shops has increased dramatically.

'Over the years, the organisation has expanded and today, with the support of a dedicated team of managers and in the region of 7,000 volunteers, we help our 25 member charities and nearly 300 guest charities to raise much-needed funds' says Christine Holland, chief executive. She continues to note that, in the past five years, charities have received over £20 million from Cards for Good Causes for the sales of their Christmas cards.

Demonstrating that each CSO is unique

For individual charities, marketing is essential to differentiate one charity from another and to help identify and sell the uniqueness of any organisation. This might be that a charity operates in Newcastle as opposed to another that only serves the Manchester area, or that one organisation

7

Although the term **unique selling proposition** comes from the commercial world, the concept and variations of it can be applied in the not-for-profit sector. Typically, USP is about what makes a product or a service unique to differentiate it in a way that customers will want to buy it over its competitors. While this is relevant to many CSOs, the term can be extended and modified in the sector; for example, volunteers can be seen as charities' 'unique benefit proposition'. See Chapter 6 for more about this.

provides information to the public as opposed to another that campaigns for change by local or national government. Only by stressing this, its USP – unique selling proposition – can any charity expect to gain competitive advantage, and as this chapter will further explain, a myriad of other external pressures mean that many CSOs without a competitive advantage will be doomed to fail in the twenty-first century. Provided that this pressure leads to mergers that have net resulting increases for beneficiaries, this could be a positive one. The danger remains, however, that volunteer trustees become discouraged, the charity closes and the net impact is a reduction in services offered.

Higher-education establishments are an interesting case when it comes to using marketing to differentiate one establishment from the next. As not-for-profit organisations that are fee- and grant-driven but often with large development departments to generate additional voluntary income for capital projects, they are well placed to integrate marketing through those development functions. After all, they are looking to the future of the establishment – what research, course development and future services the organisation will offer and how it will deliver those services strategically (in short, the full marketing mix). All too often, however, universities and schools accept their brands as given and simply regard development as the means to this end. This is perhaps where such

Marketing mix is a term used to describe the choices that an organisation must make in the process of getting services or products to market, i.e. the organisation's 'offering'. It can be seen as being synonymous with the four Ps (or, in this book, the five Ps): price, product, promotion, place and *position* (see page 36).

establishments differ from high-profile, cause-based charities. Many educational establishments rely on differentiating themselves and pursuing excellence only in particular niches. Yet they have the ability, when they choose to use it, to harness marketing to drive development and fuel the future.

For example, the Central School of Speech and Drama in London has very clear, well-stated aims to 'reach out, promoting excellence and building on a reputation that is already second to none', said the School's previous development director, Verity Haines. She noted the need to 'line all the soldiers up' before going public with any fundraising activity. She added, 'the school has a unique opportunity to market its future courses to a worldwide audience. But it'll only work if, through good marketing, we've established who those potential attendees are and how we talk to them effectively.' She observed that the school could work independently but also collaborate with other organisations that might otherwise be seen as competitors (personal communication, 2002).

Economic pressures and issues of public confidence

The mergers outlined above are but one consequence of a growing suspicion among the British public that not-for-profit groups are no longer the blameless, efficient organisations they were once assumed to be. High-profile scandals involving the misappropriation and misuse of funds, 'big business' marketing and fundraising techniques, and a general cynicism in the media where good-news stories are no longer of interest have all conspired to reduce public confidence in the sector.

Other mergers are driven more by economic pressures. In October 2011, for example, it was announced that No Smoking Day was to merge with the British Heart Foundation in March 2012 in an effort to secure its future following a 50% cut in funding due to government cuts.

Against this background, not-for-profit organisations are being forced to become more transparent about their operations and their respective costs, explaining why investment in fundraising and promotion is essential if organisations are to survive and continue to serve the individuals and groups who have come to rely on them. This requires a greater understanding of the public's attitudes and concerns, so that appropriate marketing and communication strategies can be developed. Increasingly, not-for-profit organisations are signing up to specialist omnibus surveys, such as those offered by Fund Ratios and the Charity Monitor, to check and understand the changing landscape of public attitudes, behaviour and perceptions.

There is also the supposed phenomenon of 'donor fatigue'. Opinion is divided as to whether this is a real or purely theoretical phenomenon. It is, perhaps, most likely that people are simply tired of being asked repeatedly and inappropriately. Nevertheless, recent years have seen the overall value of donations to UK charities broadly stagnating (Dobbs et al. 2012) and the double dip recession, online gambling and the National Lottery cannot be totally to blame. The public is not diverting its donations out of individual charities and into the Lottery or other umbrella appeals. The money normally given is perhaps being diverted into expenditure on homes, on entertainment and holidays, and, increasingly, on the cost of care for parents and grandparents in later life. This is probably evidenced by the downturn in the value of charitable legacies seen by a number of charities in the last few years (Clark et al. 2012).

Only by reminding the public that charitable giving is a vital element of modern society can fundraising organisations hope to expand the overall pot of money available to the sector. Without that, charities will be forced to rob Peter to pay Paul, fighting among themselves for dwindling financial resources. There have been attempts in the past to run generic marketing campaigns promoting the 'giving is good' message and further work in this area is already underway. For example, an earlier initiative spearheaded by the National Council for Voluntary Organisations (NCVO) and the Institute of Fundraising resulted in the Giving Campaign. The re-branding of Gift Aid helped public awareness, although it is fair to say that the overall campaign did not have a marked effect on levels of charitable giving. Perhaps more successful has been the Remember a Charity campaign which aims to persuade those making a will to mention their favourite causes in their wills. A more detailed discussion of this and the linked legacy campaign follows in Chapter 7. The Funding Commission, also spearheaded by the NCVO, was reported in the *Funding the Future* report in December 2010 and the implications of this report for the future of giving are discussed in Chapter 10.

Taking on the private sector and contracts

It would be wholly wrong to suggest that competition for charities can come only from other fundraising and voluntary organisations. A large number of charities are involved in the delivery of direct services to disabled people, those with terminal illnesses, animals, and other groups. Leonard Cheshire Disability, for example, delivers respite care, domiciliary services, day-centre places, and long-term residential care and employment services. Many of these services are delivered under contracts with local social services departments, and there are many other not-for-profit and for-profit organisations that are delivering similar services and competing for the same contracts in many areas of the UK.

Not only does this mean that USPs must again come into play, but charities must also adapt their practices to meet the strict requirements levied by local government departments. It is a fallacy to believe that contracts are awarded on price alone, although this is certainly a very significant factor and one with which some charities are struggling to cope. The way in which an organisation's services – its products – are packaged and presented is critical in securing a successful partnership with the public sector, and it is equally important that any competing charity understands the requirements and demands of its client. When tendering for contracts, it is important to remember that, at that particular point in time, the client is the body offering the contract, not the individual user who will ultimately receive the service. However, the demise of Southern Cross (a very large commercial provider of care services) in 2011 demonstrates, among other things, the risks of depending solely on one source of income. Southern Cross depended almost entirely on local authority contracts to provide care for residents and when it lost some contracts, after poor standards in some homes were discovered, it was tipped into insolvency.

Quality and standards are vitally important here, values which, when clearly in evidence, can be powerful marketing tools. Services must be monitored and evaluated properly, ensuring that the requirements of contractors are continually met, if not exceeded. If the charity is to deliver on all expectations, this also demands a regular dialogue with the contract-

> **Relationship fundraising** is a term originally made popular by Ken Burnett in his book entitled *Relationship Fundraising*, first published in 1992. A few years after the publication of his book he stated: 'Relationship fundraising is just a currently fashionable piece of jargon. It could just as easily be called 'donor care', or 'supporter development', or 'donor loyalty' or whatever. They would all do equally well' (Burnett 1996a).

ing organisation and with service users or their families. Contracts always come with a renewal date and a charity that forgets this and allows a service, once awarded, to decline, will almost inevitably lose the contract the next time around. As in any area in which it is employed, marketing must be seen as a long-term exercise, not a short-term fix.

Keeping the customer satisfied

In the previous section, emphasis was given to considering the needs of the contractor of a charitable service. However, end-users, whether they are customers or supporters (not necessarily beneficiaries), are just as impor-tant for CSOs as they are for commercial retailers and other sales- and marketing-driven companies. It follows, therefore, that, as the not-for-profit sector expands and becomes more competitive, the requirements of these customers and supporters must be taken into full account. It is, inci-dentally, the author's profound belief that 'donors' give blood and body parts, and so hereafter people who give cash to charities will be referred to simply as 'givers'.

The concept of 'relationship fundraising' is no longer new to char-ities, and in fact has been practised by some organisations for many years. As long ago as the early 1990s, Barnardo's wrote to all of its regular direct-mail givers and asked them how often they would like to hear from the charity each year. By treating them as individuals, Barnardo's success-fully reduced unwanted direct mail, thus saving on costs, and saw a corresponding uplift in the value of donations from its grateful supporters. There followed some pioneering work by Lawrence Stroud on behalf of Botton Village, a community of people with severe learning difficulties. Addressing a workshop at the National Fundraising Convention in Birmingham in 1995, Stroud made the point that by consistently asking givers what information they wanted and how often they wanted it, the charity enjoyed remarkable response rates from the giver database. Other organisations – such as Greenpeace and the NSPCC – have followed suit,

Customer relationship marketing has the same focus on care, development and loyalty as relationship fundraising. It is an approach that prioritises getting to know customers and winning their loyalty. This is based on the idea that customers can only be targeted effectively by forming a relationship with each individual.

asking their supporters what it is they want to know, and tailoring their approaches and communications accordingly.

Supermarkets and banks are increasingly using these same techniques under the headings of customer relationship marketing and customer-centric marketing and the discerning member of the public is coming to expect to be treated as an individual, rather than just an entry on a database. There are further benefits also to the charity, in that it costs far more to recruit a new giver than it does to service an existing supporter and keep them loyal to the organisation. While a new giver, recruited through what is probably, at best, a break-even cold mailing and more usually a very significant investment, may become a valuable supporter over time, existing supporters can provide a more immediate financial return if treated correctly.

There is, however, a limit to the extent to which any charity can call a supporter 'its own'. What has become evident in recent years is that giver loyalty does not mean giver monogamy. Many individuals will support a basket of charities, perhaps giving a regular amount to two or three and more occasional donations to several others. The same phenomenon can be seen in individual retailing habits, where stores are chosen depending on their current offers and availability and consumers boast of a number of store cards in their wallets and purses. Indeed the latest response to this 'customer promiscuity' is for some of the major players to issue a joint loyalty or bonus card called Nectar. On the Internet, few, if any, websites have the exclusive attention of surfers, though individuals may choose from a selection of personally selected favourites. When a charity's closest supporters may also be making donations to indirect, if not direct, competitors, principles of customer care are vitally important if individuals are not to take their business and their donations entirely elsewhere.

Interestingly, opportunities abound wherever there is change. The House of Commons Library confirms that the population is ageing rapidly (Cracknell 2010). This is clearly a marketing opportunity for companies which aim products and services at older people (see Chapter 9, page 132 for a discussion of the nature of the baby boomers). CSOs which direct services at the elderly will see increasing demands upon their resources. But where are the joint ventures to fund such growth? For example, various attempts have been made to establish lists of reputable plumbers and builders for vulnerable people living alone (or indeed anyone desperate for a reliable service) but an endorsement by a charity that works directly with older people would enormously enhance the reputation and brand of such a service provider. Linked programmes between such companies and charities, however, are conspicuous by their absence.

Making staff and volunteers matter

This competition for individual supporters doesn't just focus on potential givers and other fundraising supporters, or even on those bodies that contract for charitable services. Another story of dwindling resources and increased competition can be told of staff and volunteer recruitment, where many organisations, both large and small, face crisis. This is particularly true for those charities whose personnel are responsible for delivering services as opposed to fundraising or more administrative support.

There are a number of reasons for this increased competition. In terms of recruiting staff, charities are always up against commercial organisations that can pay higher salaries and offer more attractive benefits in terms of paid holiday, health insurance and pension contributions. This is less of a problem when recruiting specialist staff, such as fundraisers, as the competition is only between charities and other organisations involved in that area. But when recruiting care staff and those with the management expertise to oversee them, there are always commercial providers seeking similarly strong candidates to fill these posts. In such situations the perks and benefits on offer might well influence a candidate's decision.

An inherent advantage for CSOs, which a good marketing strategy can help to exploit, is their closeness to the individuals whom they serve. This is not to suggest that commercial providers are only out to make a profit – although this has to be the principal factor for them   but that charities have a unique understanding of the needs of their service users. More forward-thinking organisations are placing service-user representatives on their trustee boards and in other positions at the top of their organisation. This empathy with the needs of service users can help to inspire and motivate existing staff, and also to attract new staff who are drawn to a career in service delivery because of their beliefs. There are few individuals who would seek a job in the not-for-profit sector for the money alone.

Empathy is even more important when recruiting volunteers. These people are not driven at all by financial gain but instead may wish to give something back to the community in which they have prospered, or to develop new skills they are unable to practise in their regular paid employment. As with givers, volunteers are faced with a bewildering choice of charities to which they can give their time, and so any organisation must work hard to understand what prospective volunteers are seeking as well as to match those needs with what the charity itself can offer. Competition here comes not just from other charities. Any individual with time to spare has a number of opportunities before them: taking up a new hobby, fitting in freelance work, spending more time with their family, and many other options, so it is certainly not a given that volunteering is top of their list. However, with an effective market-ing campaign, charities can raise awareness within their own organisation of both volunteering per se and volunteering opportunities specifically.

With regard to their training, team development and morale-building priorities, for-profit organisations that ignore the opportunity of working with voluntary and community organisations do so at their peril. Exam-ples of coordinated staff-volunteering abound, as do the reports of improved team working, job satisfaction and increased productivity. Marks & Spencer, for example, actively encourages staff to work, singly or in small teams, as volunteers on a wide range of community projects. They report significant successes from both employer and employee perspectives. The John Lewis Partnership practises even more participation and offers all permanent employees the opportunity to become a limited liability partner and to share in the profits. The organisation is, thus, far more of a social enterprise than a commercial enterprise such as Tesco or Sainsbury.

The positive encouragement by B&Q of the employment of older and disabled staff resulted directly in greater employee loyalty, particularly at a local level where a team spirit can be significantly enhanced. Personal communications with the company's corporate responsibility staff in 2001 revealed that staff turnover had fallen and morale had been improved. An additional benefit from this has been an increase in staff volunteering projects, perhaps because of the wider existing community involvement of those older staff members.

In a similar way, charities can use staff to achieve multiple object-ives; they can augment fundraising activities and at the same time build an internal understanding of those very fundraising needs. For example, a number of non-fundraising staff at Leonard Cheshire took part in an overseas challenge event to 'walk the volcanoes' in Nicaragua and succeeded in raising several thousand pounds of additional income for overseas projects. Importantly, however, they also built greater internal understanding of the fundraising needs and priorities in an organisation that employs 7,000 staff mostly on the service-delivery side (personal communication, 2000). Shared values and greater understanding were the end result. The beneficial effects upon the organisations that adopt such practices can reach much further and multiply when such activities bring together two non-competitive organisations: Tesco adopted Alzheimer's Society and Alzheimer Scotland as its Charity of the Year in 2011. This involved staff and customers in more than 4,000 fundraising events, including trekking up Mount Kilimanjaro (Lombard 2012). This empha-sis on people can enable a company to achieve benefits from working with a charity that extend far beyond those of simple altruism and philanthropy.

Case study: The Mitie Group and Macmillan Cancer

The Mitie Group is a leading FTSE 250 business with over 70,000 people and revenues in excess of £2 billion (Mitie 2012). It is a disparate group of companies that provide facilities management around the UK and into Europe. While enjoying highly profitable growth, before 2002 Mitie had experienced significant internal communications problems and a lack of staff involvement with, or ownership of, the group's overall objectives. However, the group found huge success with its adoption of Macmillan Cancer over three years. Working closely with Mitie's human resources team, Macmillan Cancer organised a nationwide series of events, challenges and project work. This included bowling competitions that pitted Mitie group companies and teams against one another. As well as being the main fundraising vehicle, the competitions achieved huge improvements in inter-company knowledge and staff morale. These benefits, to paraphrase John Urquhart (then corporate relations director of the Mitie Group plc), could not have happened without the charity's active involvement and participation (Green 2002). This clearly demonstrates the win–win possibilities of a successful joint venture when communications and marketing objectives are clearly understood by both participants.

Conclusion

Commercial organisations tend to plan marketing as an integrated part of their overall strategy; brand development fits into this tight framework and the resulting plans dovetail neatly together even if they don't always work. By contrast, charities tend to act in a more ad hoc way, adding marketing to the fundraising and communications function so that plans are made almost as an afterthought. Even where rigorous planning is executed, in some of the larger CSOs marketing considerations tend to follow the communications strategy rather than dictate them.

It is clear from the examples outlined in this chapter that for-profit organisations can benefit hugely from cooperation with CSOs and similarly CSOs can benefit from for-profit organisations, over and above the obvious fundraising objectives.

Commercial organisations are learning that competitive advantage can be gained by directing marketing effort – not just community affairs budgets – towards active work with charities. Benefits accrue both internally and externally – internally from better communications and morale, reduced staff turnover and more productive teams with higher loyalty and championing of the brand. Externally, customers identify more closely with a favourable brand and may be more loyal while other stakeholders such as investors are equally likely to be more favourably disposed. In turn, CSOs are beginning to understand the need to consider their own marketing priorities when building strategic plans, as opposed to grafting marketing activities onto existing fundraising programmes. There is, however, much more that can be done on both sides.

CHAPTER TWO

A brief history of marketing

No Destitute Child Ever Refused Admission.
Dr Barnardo

Half the money I spend on advertising is wasted: the trouble is I don't know which half.
Viscount Leverhulme

Looking back over the twentieth century (and, in a few relevant instances, earlier) this chapter explores how CSOs, in particular, have increasingly come to rely on marketing methods and practice and draws direct parallels with commercial marketeers through the decades. Beginning with some of the early pioneering work of Barnardo's, and later Oxfam, it will show how marketing has evolved into today's practices and points to how it might go so much further.

Perspectives

In the nineteenth century, charities such as Barnardo's appealed directly to the public's existing value systems. Advertisements were placed in newspapers such as *The Times* to appeal to the middle and upper classes who, it was hoped, possessed both the capacity and propensity to give to the less well-off – especially when the cause was needy children.

In contrast, by the 1920s and 1930s, American commercial advertisers learned how consumers could be encouraged to identify with products and services via sponsorship. The first soap operas were just that – continuing radio sagas of everyday life/loves/dramas that were paid for, through sponsorship, by washing powder and soap manufacturers. People's aspirations towards particular lifestyles were recognised by those marketeers and their advertising agencies and much of the scripting, while not yet making use of overt product placement, certainly gave rise to the links that advertisers today seek to create in their own scripts, graphics and storytelling.

The development of professional marketing

Once the power of advertising and public relations had been grasped, mainly by fast-moving consumer goods manufacturers in the 1920s, it was only a question of time before academics started studying the subject, and by the 1960s research into consumer behaviour was a recognised discipline.

In the UK, the Sales Managers Association was first formed in May 1911. In 1931 the name of this Association's magazine was changed to reflect the much wider subject area it covered – *Marketing*. It took until 1961, and much debate, to change the organisation's name to the Institute of Marketing and Sales Management. Finally, in 1968 the name became simply the Institute of Marketing and in 1989 the institute was awarded its charter mark and is now the Chartered Institute of Marketing (CIM 2012).

CIM's integrated approach to marketing training has applicability to social marketing (see page 3, Chapter 1) and, therefore, means that CSO recruiters who are seeking well-qualified marketeers can be confident that CIM Members will demonstrate a well-grounded understanding of their organisation's needs. While the successful study of social marketing can demonstrate academic achievement and rigorous research, this must be matched with a pragmatic understanding that comes from practical experience. This experience may also be found in such commercial marketeers (CIM Members must have a minimum of three years in marketing, including one year in a management role).

The beginnings of targeting techniques

The early work of Harold Sumption, George Smith, et al. built on successful newspaper advertisement appeals where the use of simple typography and layout gave rise to the impression of a rushed, cheaply done job conveying an urgent message that requires an immediate response (Allford 1993). The technique was not confined to newspaper advertising but instead began to be used in direct mail, initially to existing supporters but soon to lists of targeted individuals who, it was thought, might share the same concerns and values as those who had already proven their interest.

Segmenting a supporter list using **RFV** is done by working out when a giver last interacted with an organisation (recency), how many interactions the giver had with the organisation over a given time (frequency) and individual donation amount (value). This technique can be used, for example, to streamline direct mail campaigns by helping an organisation to identify which givers are most likely to support the organisation. The aim of this is to reduce the number of inappropriate direct mail recipients and therefore mailing costs by a considerable amount, without losing potential regular and high-value givers, thereby keeping the vast majority of income.

Such work was crude by today's sophisticated targeting techniques. Attributes such as recency, frequency and value (RFV) had yet to be identified as ways of segmenting giver lists, and predictors of likely behaviour and lifestyle lists had seen little development. Nevertheless, the application of such marketing techniques worked wonderfully well and response rates in double-figure percentages to cold mailings were not unusual.

Practitioners such as Oxfam's Guy Stringer began to wonder if greater use could not be made of such successful practices, without compromising core values and integrity (personal communication, George Smith, 2001). In the face of trustee ignorance (if not actual hostility), however, few other charities at that time in the 1970s made much headway and only began to adopt, piecemeal, marketing practices that had been seen to work. These were rarely imbued with a corporate understanding of where such strategies would lead.

Realising the importance of CSO branding

The British Rheumatism and Arthritis Association (BRA), which had been formed in 1947 by a remarkable young man named Arthur Mainwaring-Bowen, was perhaps one of the first charities to demonstrate some understanding of brand values. Waring (as he was known), had been diagnosed with Ankylosing Spondylitis (a particularly painful form of arthritis affecting the spine) and decided that, in the absence of useful user information for people with arthritis, he would form a lay organisation to help provide information and support.

By 1983 the organisation had grown very considerably, helping thousands of people with arthritis and employing a small but very active professional team aided by hundreds of volunteers, themselves often people with arthritis. However, the name had become a hindrance to further expansion and understanding of the organisation's mission. Confusion around the medical terms and the actual work of the charity abounded because there was no clear indication of the organisation's work in its name. Indeed many thought it a professional association for rheumatologists. Despite misgivings and apprehension, the trustees accepted the need and agreed to change the name to Arthritis Care. This, in the early 1980s, nicely espoused a punchy yet caring ethos that said, very simply, 'this is a charity that cares for people with arthritis and provides support for them'.

BRA never funded medical research. That activity was, unusually for medically orientated charities, the remit of a completely separate charity – the Arthritis and Rheumatism Council – which has now also changed its name to the Arthritis Research Campaign, retaining its well-known acronym (ARC). This change shows some understanding of the public's propensity to trust a name that it recognises. Arthritis and research are both words the general public will recognise and therefore assume that they have already heard of a charity called Arthritis Research: in the same way, most people believe there is a charity called simply, Cancer Research (of which Cancer Research UK cleverly took ownership).

> **Prompted brand awareness** is used to find out how effective brand promotion is. It is measured by asking a sample number of people individually whether they recognise a specific brand – in this case, a charity name (usually as part of a list) – after either hearing the charity name said aloud or seeing the name and/or logo.

After the changes, Arthritis Care entered a decade of strong growth through a rapid expansion of its branch structure (all run by volunteers) and membership that peaked in the mid-1990s at more than 70,000. While marketing had not necessarily been accepted as a complete function within the organisation, the practices involved in brand management, including defining, positioning and delivering the brand, and the need to foster understanding through effective public relations had been successfully employed. By 2003 prompted brand awareness had never been higher (see Chapter 4: 'The charity as a brand'). Unfortunately, whilst a successful policy agenda continued to be pursued, over the next decade progressive disinvestment in the hotels and branches, together with large cuts in fundraising, led to a dramatic decline in income. For the year ending 31st December 2011 total income at £4.8 million, was less than half of the 2000 level.

Commercial case study: HSBC

When the Hong Kong and Shanghai Bank (HSBC) acquired the Midland Bank, one of the four major high street banks in the UK, it was looking for growth – expanding sales, increasing market share and generating greater profitability.

Many were very wary of the impact such a takeover would have. The Midland had several hundred thousand loyal (well, at least long-term) customers who liked the philosophy captured in the friendly smiling Griffin (the Midland logo at that time) with the strapline, 'the listening bank'. Everything that HSBC has done has retained that basic belief and attitude. The griffin went and the red double triangle appeared. Then the name went and HSBC appeared with the double triangle. But core beliefs remained consistent. Advertising in the summer of 2011 still talked of HSBC as the world's local bank, implying that it is still there, listening and ready to act for you the customer.

This is a particularly useful example of an international organisation understanding and building upon the existing reputation, brand awareness and customers' beliefs about that brand.

Past examples of the limitations of market research

On 4 September 1957, Ford in the USA introduced the first car said to have been designed and brought to market using extensive market research, although how much was actually used and how much discarded is subject to debate. Designers created a classic 1950s saloon car – with big tail fins and sculpted looks that were high on luxury – and endeavoured to provide a feel-good factor for both men (identified as the prime buyers) and women (seen as secondary decision influencers). It was called the 'Edsel' after Henry Ford's son.

The car was launched amidst a barrage of advertising and press comment. Sadly, despite the intention to satisfy customer needs (in this case to bring to market at the right price the car that a vast number of American families would buy and enjoy owning), it failed spectacularly.

One theory about its failure concerns the shortcomings of the research brief. What researchers didn't include (and at the time could be forgiven for not considering) was a forward prediction as to the likes and dislikes of American society 12 months and two years after the car's launch. What happened? On the 4 October 1957 the Russians launched Sputnik, the first man-made orbital satellite, and America realised it had lost that round of the space race. In turn, the complacency that had characterised the late 1950s in the USA turned to a new era of, if not austerity, then certainly realism and a desire to regain the lead in world technology. Tastes changed almost overnight. Overt opulence was out, efficiency, more austere lines and modest fittings characterised the cars of the next decade. Tail fins were dead and the Edsel died with them.

Whatever the real reasons for the radical shift in American tastes and behaviour, it showed that market research is only part of the picture. Marketeers were still learning.

The often-cited 'New Coke' failure demonstrates a later example of the limitations of market research. Coca-Cola launched a newly formulated version of its flagship brand in 1985 following a market research project (one of the biggest in history) that found, quite clearly, that people preferred the taste of this newly formulated Coca-Cola to the old one and also to its main rival, Pepsi (blind taste tests had previously put Pepsi on top). Although the right questions were asked and the market research was conducted correctly, management failed to recognise the strength of the original brand. In short, even though the majority of people preferred the taste of this new cola, they were so attached and wedded to the traditional Coca-Cola flagship brand that, ultimately, they were unwilling to betray that loyalty (Schindler 1992).

A more recent example of marketing research

Case study: Leonard Cheshire

Early in the twenty-first century, Leonard Cheshire was faced with huge potential changes in the market for care services for disabled people and, in particular, residential services for disabled people. It conducted a wide-ranging, 12-month review of its activities and resources together with commissioned external marketing research from Ashridge Business School. The review was in response to the government's introduction from April 2002 of new residential care standards that, for the first time ever, differentiated between the standards required for disabled people and the frail elderly.

During the previous 40 years, the charity had built up a huge range of residential services ranging from large rambling country houses to small state-of-the-art supported-living units where every resident has their own front door. Some 120 buildings were involved and for the first time the charity discovered that it was the market leader in providing residential care for disabled people. It also learned that, if it were to modernise all its residential places (and market indicators pointed towards an overall similar requirement for places over ten years though with increasing levels of support), it would need to invest up to £100 million over the next five years. As a result, a complete strategic review of all the charity's operations was completed and a new strategic plan developed. This outlines a clear example of how marketing research can drive strategic planning. Rising to that challenge was to prove very difficult but by 2010, with more clarity and planning, the charity's turnover had grown to £155 million.

Marketing practices

There is nothing new within most marketing practices. An example of direct marketing can be seen in the brush salesmen who were selling door-to-door in the early twentieth century. What is different is the use that charities, in particular, make of these practices, often excelling in their execution and getting response rates that are the envy of the commercial sector. In 2004/05, when the Brooke Hospital for Animals (now called simply 'the Brooke') began to ask its 20,000 loyal supporters for regular donations it enjoyed response rates in excess of 30%. Similarly, early cold mailings to carefully selected lists of those already interested in animal welfare returned better than 10%.

Redmond Mullin commented that some of St Paul's letters to the Corinthians are among the best fundraising letters ever written (personal communication 2002). In these letters St Paul appeals to the Corinthians to collect money to send to Jerusalem for famine relief. He encourages regular giving by asking them to set aside a proportion of their income each week and emphasises the importance of Christian generosity and equality. He compares the Corinthians' situation with others in other countries, where they are already giving in this way and yet their inhabitants are much poorer than they. The number of fundraising techniques used in these letters alone is impressive (SOFII 2010).

Two thousand years on, this perhaps indicates that there really is very little new under the sun. Nothing new, perhaps, but there is always an opportunity to refine practices, find a new twist or use techniques in an innovative way.

The enormous growth of face-to-face canvassing – the use of paid fundraisers to ask people in the street to sign a monthly direct debit there and then – has enabled many larger well-known charities to dramatically increase their databases of regular givers. Moreover, the profile of these new supporters tends to be far younger than that of traditional responders to direct mail (PFRA 2012).

Concerns voiced by local authorities and commentators that the technique is too intrusive have led to the formation of the Public Fundraising Regulatory Authority (PFRA). While the organisation has had its work cut out managing the process of self-regulation and media criticism, it has had some notable success. For example, face-to-face agencies, which conduct the canvassing, and their charity clients have enrolled with the PFRA which enables the PFRA to monitor and regulate while local authorities can license sites with some confidence that operators will not 'flood' areas. Furthermore, the expansion of face-to-face fundraising to include house-to-house and event canvasses as well as those that are street-based means that there is a more diverse range of interventions and opportunities for dialogue.

The PFRA has appointed advocates who champion the good practice in the face of media criticism. While it is not universally liked or understood, canvassing continues to offer charities the opportunity to engage with givers at a much earlier age than has ever been possible with direct mail, advertising and other direct-response techniques.

The limits of marketing

Marketing cannot provide all the answers. Too often organisations have turned to marketing to help them through difficult times. Poor product take-up is seen as a failure of advertising rather than necessarily of poor design, distribution or pricing. Marketing can help identify needs and ways to fulfil them but it isn't the complete picture, although many marketing directors might have you believe that it is. That must be the role of the organisation's overall strategy and should flow from its core vision and mission. This is examined further in Chapter 3.

Most marketing texts analyse the constituent elements of marketing into the four Ps, though many go further. For example, Ian Bruce (2011) defines the usual terms – Product, Promotion, Price and Place – plus four more: People, Physical evidence, Process and Philosophy. An in-depth discussion of the four main Ps starts on page 36 in Chapter 3. However, a fifth P, Position, will also be discussed as it is so important that it can usefully be considered as a vital element of the overall mix (see pp. 42–43).

In reality, marketing can be segmented into many more elements and so is not simply a matter of identifying the Ps, whether four, five, eight or more. An understanding of this totality and its effective application is what defines successful marketeers.

As will be discussed further in Chapter 3, market and marketing research are very important aspects of defining the market needs and an organisation's ability to meet them. Sometimes, however, the best research in the world cannot predict events.

Conclusion

Good marketing people can always construct, add or design a new twist to old methods of fundraising. Face-to-face fundraising by canvassers in the street is not, in itself, a new idea. Volunteers have been conducting collections for decades. The advent of the direct debit, so that supporters pledge, typically, £5 or £10 per month – Gift Aided – rather than put 50p or £1 in the collecting tin or envelope has, however, revolutionised the technique. Despite much criticism and debate from the media which even call canvassers 'chuggers' (charity muggers), charities continue to find this a very cost-effective way of recruiting younger givers.

Crucially, organisations have learned that they need to build their brand by investing across the marketing mix and across all audiences. That is, they invest precious resources in each of the marketing elements such as promotion, pricing and positioning in addition to more basic questions of products, services, distribution and target market segments. Chapter 3 looks at this in greater detail. In order for there to be coherence in brand development, however, the most important single requirement is for an integrated marketing strategy to be developed, agreed and implemented. The next chapter considers all the necessary steps.

CHAPTER THREE

Preparing a marketing strategy

> *When you see the correct course, act; do not wait for orders.*
> Sun Tzu

> *Good plans shape good decisions. That's why good planning helps to make elusive dreams come true.*
> Lester Bittel

Today, marketing is an acknowledged constituent of nearly all organisations, including all but the smallest charities or one-person businesses. However, for many, especially within the not-for-profit sector, marketing is still very much regarded as an add-on, a luxury even, or perhaps as a function that is bolted on alongside fundraising and communications rather than an integral part of an organisation's overall vision and mission. This chapter explains why a clear marketing strategy must come first. It outlines the essential elements of a strategy and shows how that strategy must be grounded in the organisation's own mission and strategic objectives.

Strategy

Redmond Mullin (2002) reminds us that 'strategy' is originally a military concept and he illustrates the hierarchy of levels between planning and execution as shown in figure 3.1.

FIGURE 3.1 PLANNING PROCESS HIERARCHY

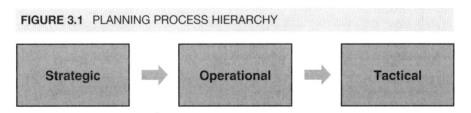

Dwight Eisenhower had something to say about the planning process: 'In preparing for battle I have always found that plans are useless, but planning is indispensable.' From this statement it can be inferred that, in an environment of constantly changing circumstances, it is essential to be flexible and to be able to react effectively to these changes. In this way, specific plans may be useless. However, the planning process is crucial –

the act of considering what the risks and opportunities will be allows an army, or a business or charity, to be properly prepared. Also in the military context, Clausewitz stated in *Vom Kriege*, originally published in 1832 and translated as *On War*, that 'in strategy everything is very simple, but not on that account very easy'. To expand a little on this, it is 'the means and forms which strategy uses', he states, that are extremely simple, even if those in the academic world speak of it with 'high-flown emphasis'. It is in understanding moral forces that it becomes more difficult, and the carrying out of the plan 'without being obliged to deviate from it a thousand times by a thousand varying influences, requires, besides great strength of character, great clearness and steadiness of mind' (Clausewitz 1873). In this way, Clausewitz's view on the execution of the plan may appear to diverge from Eisenhower's statement, but being guided steadily by the plan, yet having the flexibility to deviate where necessary, and not being constantly swayed by innumerable influences, may be the key to carrying out a plan effectively.

Strategic management

The process of strategic management and planning includes:

• the analysis and identification of strategic goals (through clarification of and agreement to the vision, mission and strategic objectives) in relation to the internal and external environment of an organisation;

• the taking of decisions about the overall direction of the organisation and in particular the areas in which it should operate in order to create competitive and sustainable advantages in the market;

• the actions that an organisation must undertake to achieve its objectives including making the resources available to implement the policies and strategies to achieve those objectives successfully.

It also includes the competitive analysis of why some organisations outperform others and seeks to integrate, as far as possible, the various organisational activities such as marketing, fundraising and sales to assist the achievement of organisational goals.

Igor Ansoff (1918–2001) is known as the father of strategic management and was one of the first academics to recognise the need for the concept. In his seminal work *Corporate Strategy* (1965) he simplified this concept into two sentences:

1. The key to strategy is recognizing that if a company is functioning, it is part of the environment.

2. When a Manager understands the environment and recognizes that the environment is constantly changing, then the manager can make the correct decisions in leading the organisation into the future.

Ansoff 1968

Dr Ansoff (1968) theorised that if a company becomes purely self-serving, it soon loses track of its direction and dies. He believed that long-term profitability results from a commitment to understanding the political and social fabric of a community. This is an important consideration that underlines the need to ensure that for-profit organisations work together with not-for-profit organisations to achieve these mutual objectives. It was an early indication that corporate responsibility should be an integral part of a company's strategy and not just a reaction to public opinion. Ideally strategic management and planning becomes a continual process.

The reasons behind this continual process are manifold. As David Saint, chair of Action Planning said, 'the pressure to plan strategically often comes from fundraisers who are expected to quantify their plans; charities often act intuitively – they are effective – but the direction isn't written down, so how can fundraisers be clear about their planning environment?' Saint went on to state that 'open conversations with chief executives are crucial to establish a strategic planning framework. Indeed without mentioning marketing the strategic plan can be the Trojan horse by which marketing can be introduced' (personal interview 2002).

Integration of the marketing strategy into overall strategy

For marketing to be effective in an organisation, a marketing approach needs to permeate the entire management board and, for that matter, the whole board of trustees or directors. Only when an organisation can embrace all the disciplines, necessitated by a marketing-led approach, will the benefits start to manifest themselves.

A marketing strategy, therefore, must be clear and demonstrate that it is in agreement with overall organisational goals. Furthermore, this strategy must grow out of and reflect the organisation's vision and mission. It seems unlikely, then, that a stand-alone marketing strategy, however well planned and executed, would achieve all that it should towards enabling an organisation to fulfil its overall objectives.

The relation of the organisation's vision to its strategic objectives

It may be helpful to use the analogy of the American space programme. The *vision*, the crucial ultimate goal for going into space was 'To reach the stars'. Following President Kennedy's challenge in 1961 in response to the Russian lead in the space race, NASA set itself the *mission*, which was to get a manned spacecraft to the moon (and safely back again) before the end of that decade. The strategic plan was the progressive programme of Mercury, Gemini, and Apollo with eventually Apollo 11 landing on the moon on 20 July 1969. Armstrong, Aldrin and Shepherd returned home safely a week later. Each part of the mission had specific objectives; achievable aims against which progress could be measured. The vision remains but that particular part of the mission was achieved successfully.

Crucially then, CSOs have to espouse a clear vision – the big picture – from which an achievable mission can be derived and only then can meaningful strategic objectives and the marketing strategy be developed. This process is like that of targeting (see figure 3.2), remembering that one is focusing down to the objectives which inevitably can only ever be a small part of the overall picture. This is somewhat different from the conventional view that often portrays the vision in the centre of the target.

FIGURE 3.2 TARGETING THE VISION, MISSION AND STRATEGIC OBJECTIVES

Trustee and board ownership

Much of the impetus for 'vision' and 'mission' should be coming from the trustee board or board of directors, though, as we saw from the Leonard Cheshire case study in Chapter 2, the pressure to review and change may well be marketing-driven.

It is essential to have a sense of ownership of the strategy in order to enable effective marketing planning. The 'Internal communications' section on page 51 discusses internal markets and the necessary communications, but before that stage it is vital to ensure ownership not just of the overall strategic objectives but specifically of the marketing strategy and objectives.

The process necessary to involve and gain understanding from a board and to ensure its ownership of the plan will require careful consideration of the individuals involved. Understanding and acceptance by the senior management team is a crucial part of the plan. This at least will ensure that criticism or unhelpful counter-tactics from, say, financial- or service-orientated board members can be identified and resolved long before they become an issue. One of the many useful analytical tools that may be used during planning is the Boston Matrix (Stern and Stalk 1998) and the many variations that now exist (see page 47). It is particularly helpful to generalist trustees or non-executive directors who are attempting to gain an insight into the processes involved, and the need to move in a particular direction; it can be adapted for use by just about any organisation, public, private or not-for-profit.

Marketing review and assessment

The following sections outline the important distinction between market research and market*ing* research. It is helpful for these differences to be grasped and understood fully in order for the right questions to be asked and answered satisfactorily. Some do use the terms 'market research' and 'marketing research' interchangeably, but the distinction can be made usefully in order to highlight the dangers of *only* considering market research.

Market research

Market research is the consideration and examination of existing markets. It looks carefully at a market itself – the overall size, competition and potential growth. Doing market research involves systematically gathering information about this particular market and potentially segmenting customers into various groups (using models such as RFV – see page 18).

A crucial aspect of market research is not only what the market wants, or thinks it wants, but also what is already being produced – that is, the competition, the totality of the market and the relative market shares that each of the main players enjoy.

> **Market share** is the percentage of total revenue for an industry or sector that is controlled by a particular organisation (or product). **Market position** is where an organisation, brand or product sits in relation to the total market and its competitors and organisations that are offering similar activities. This may be in terms of its volume of sales relative to its competitors' sales volume, for example. It is an indication of why customers are choosing that organisation rather than a competitor.

While market research is an important tool within a strategy, the cases of the Ford Edsel and new Coke show how wrong one can be to depend upon it entirely (see page 21). That said, increasing numbers of charities are realising that specific, appropriate market research is a vital element in the development of any meaningful marketing strategy. It is important that the need for particular research is understood properly so that the right questions are asked.

The use of market research

If there is existing market research, this can be factored in to the analysis. Conversely, the need to know much more about certain aspects of key markets or audiences may underline the requirement to conduct qualitative or quantitative research. Given a clear understanding of the organisation's market position it is then possible to begin drawing up a marketing strategy which details the objectives and the actions to be taken to achieve them.

The marketing strategy restates the organisation's objectives as they relate to the marketing function, and provides a detailed set of agreed action plans to achieve those key targets. Once understood, this process can, in outline, be put together in an hour. However, for a marketing strategy to have the greatest impact it is vital to obtain agreement and hence ownership from the board and every other department which has any influence at all upon the organisation's effectiveness. In this way, the marketing strategy should be a part of the organisational strategy as shown in figure 3.3.

FIGURE 3.3 AN INTEGRATED STRATEGIC PLANNING CYCLE

Competition in the market

When considering the competition to charities in the market, it would be wholly wrong to suggest that it can come only from other fundraising and voluntary organisations. A large number of charities, for example, are involved in the delivery of direct services to disabled people. Many of these services are delivered under contract with local social services departments, and there are many other not-for-profit and for-profit organisations delivering similar services and competing for the same contracts in many areas of the UK. Thus market research must look at the entirety of a given market – however imprecise the definitions – so that realistic projections and planning criteria can be adopted.

Only by conducting rigorous market research did Leonard Cheshire, doing a strategic review, discover that not only was it a major player in the provision of residential accommodation for disabled people (which it knew) but also that it was in fact the market leader with more than 50% of the total market. This significantly influenced the organisation's analysis and planning and its resulting strategy.

More usually CSOs occupy tiny niches within much larger market segments and often feel that such research is neither appropriate nor worthwhile since market leadership is not their objective. However, a comprehensive review of every player in a chosen market or segment can be most revealing and offer opportunities for change, growth, amalgamation or partnership that would not otherwise have been envisaged. It is vital to have a clear understanding of who else is operating in the same areas, with similar or differing services, solutions or approaches. The same rigour that is taken as read in most commercial marketing departments should be applied to the planning process within CSOs.

Comparisons: market-research spending

With the implementation of an effective marketing strategy plan, charities can both raise awareness of the issues and enhance their position with chosen audiences. In order to be effective, the plan has to be grounded in thorough quantitative and qualitative research.

Figure 3.4 displays analysis of research that was commissioned by the author in 2002 and conducted by Crossbow Research. Twenty-four charities responded with incomes ranging from £10 to £100 million plus. As figure 3.4 shows, charities historically spend little on market research compared to many medium to large commercial organisations (which spend anything from 1% to 3% of turnover on market research). But charities are changing. With the production of a meaningful, integrated marketing strategy they are far more likely to generate the resources and power to achieve their stated strategic objectives. Once produced, a marketing strategy plan should feed directly into the budgeting process so that there is an automatic review process, and updating on a quarterly, six-monthly or annual basis becomes a normal part of the marketing activities. This iterative cycle is important in ensuring that plans do not get neatly bound and left on bookshelves.

Of course, the reason for this lower proportion of spending is that the majority of charities – smaller charities in particular – would, or believe they would, find it difficult to find the funds to spend on market research. With this in mind, it is possible to conduct certain types of market research in-house. For example, Richard Lee, director of marketing at the Directory of Social Change, noted that his department can make objective comparisons based on facts about its competitors' training provision with regard to the number and breadth of courses. The information can be found in various publicly available reports, and using this information the marketing department is able to find its position in the market.

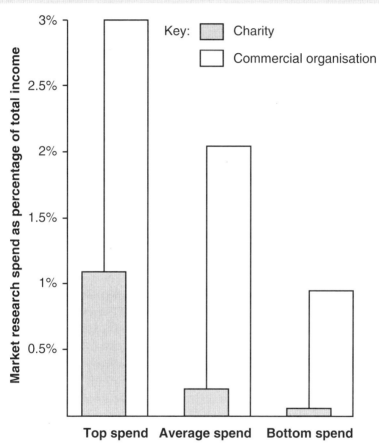

FIGURE 3.4 CHARITIES' AND COMMERCIAL ORGANISATIONS' MARKET RESEARCH SPEND AS A PERCENTAGE OF THEIR TOTAL INCOMES, SHOWING THE HIGHEST AND LOWEST SINGLE CHARITY AND COMMERCIAL ORGANISATION SPEND, AND THE AVERAGE CHARITY AND COMMERCIAL SPEND OVERALL (BATTEN 2002)

While this approach can work with this type of market research, it is more difficult with focus groups, Richard points out. If a marketing department were to conduct focus group research in-house, for example, it might unintentionally influence or lead the people in the groups by being connected to the organisation. People are not as likely to be open and honest in that situation. However, if an outside organisation conducts the research anonymously, i.e. without mentioning any connection with the organisation for which it is doing the research, this creates a more impersonal environment that encourages honest feedback (personal communication 2012).

Marketing research

While market research is about analysing particular existing markets and market trends, marketing research looks more deeply at existing and potential demand, an organisation's offering, customers' practices and aspirations and the position that an organisation should adopt or seek to move to in order to meet its strategic objectives. Indeed, the information gleaned from market research can be used and analysed in marketing research to identify what the market needs are. In short, marketing research tries to look at the whole picture.

An organisation should start by identifying its own internal strengths and weaknesses, and external opportunities and threats. Usually known as a SWOT analysis, this component is crucial in helping to identify in what direction any organisation, for-profit or not-for-profit, should be moving. The use of this and other analytic tools such as the PESTLE analysis (Political, Economic, Social, Technical, Legal and Environment factors) are examined below.

SWOT analysis

Before deciding upon new or revised objectives it is crucial to understand where the organisation is, not just in terms of the total market and its competition but also internally: how is it performing against existing plans, objectives or simple aspirations? A SWOT analysis (as shown in figure 3.5), looking inwardly at the organisation's Strengths and Weaknesses and externally at Opportunities and Threats is a useful way of examining the situation.

This always helps to focus the mind and determine many of the ingredients of the marketing mix. By charting the organisation's strengths and weaknesses (usually the internal view) and contrasting them with the opportunities and threats (generally external) it becomes clear where progress needs to be made and often indicates, in terms of marketing development, where it should be looking in terms of the Ansoff matrix, illustrated in figure 3.8, page 44. This process will help to determine, among other things, whether new services or new audiences should indeed be the highest priority. Having done this for the organisation as a whole, fundraisers may find it helpful to conduct a SWOT analysis purely for the fundraising activities. This should show up any particular incongruences or, just as important, areas of synergy between the organisation's core activities and its fundraising programmes.

Case study: Brooke Hospital for Animals

The Brooke Hospital for Animals had experienced a gradual increase in income through the late 1980s and early 1990s as a result of the activities of highly motivated volunteers and (perhaps as a result) substantial growth in legacy income. Nevertheless, expansion in its overseas work of providing free veterinary care for working horses, donkeys and mules resulted in an even more rapid growth in expenditure. As a result annual deficits rose to a peak of £2.4 million in 1999/2000. A new chief executive was appointed and a fundraising audit commissioned. The SWOT analysis of the existing fundraising operation looked like this:

FIGURE 3.5 BROOKE HOSPITAL FOR ANIMALS' 2002 SWOT ANALYSIS

STRENGTHS
- Passionate/loyal supporter database
- Significant numbers of unprompted high-value donations
- Highly motivated local volunteers

WEAKNESSES
- Very low public awareness
- No fundraising structure
- Very little trust and corporate support
- Over-dependency on legacy income

OPPORTUNITIES
- Overseas aid work presents great case studies and photos
- Huge groundswell of middle England support for animal welfare
- Existing supporters give unprompted

THREATS
- Perception of limited scope
- Reduced support by key donors
- Increased competition by larger players

Careful analysis of the strengths and opportunities helped the development of a complete fundraising strategy to build upon the huge potential growth that existed and that was, at the time, completely underutilised.

PEST or PESTLE analysis

A similar tool, which is particularly useful for examining the external environment in rather more detail, is the PEST or PESTLE analysis as shown below in figure 3.6.

FIGURE 3.6 BROOKE HOSPITAL FOR ANIMALS' 2002 PEST ANALYSIS

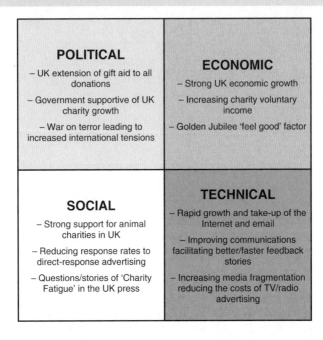

This is another valuable tool to assist boards, management groups and staff teams to examine the external factors that are likely to make an impact on an organisation over any particular time frame. For example, a marketing group may attempt to look three years forward and forecast the factors that may have an impact on their plans and, therefore, help to develop strategies to meet those changes and pressures. See also 'Forecasting the future' in Chapter 10, page 142.

Marketing planning

The Five Ps

When planning a marketing strategy it is helpful to think of the different elements – the marketing mix – that make up an organisation's offering to its chosen audiences. This helps to analyse the areas into functional responsibilities and to gain ownership of the plans and intended actions at an early opportunity, when there is still time to make meaningful changes. Traditionally these are broken into the four Ps (Product, Price, Promotion and Place) but, as will be seen, a fifth P (Position) is so important that it can be considered as a vital part of the overall mix.

In the last few years there has been an evolution in the commercial world towards consumer-centric marketing. Indeed Kotler (1999) offered an alternative to the four Ps – the four Cs. This stands for Customer value (to replace Product), Cost to the customer (Price), Convenience (Place) and Communication (Promotion). However, given the complex nature of CSOs' 'customers', which can be a mix of myriad shareholders and stakeholders (see 'Shareholder versus stakeholder', page 73), making use of the five Ps remains the more appropriate choice for the sector. This is not to say that lessons from consumer-centric marketing must not be learned and used by the sector, and indeed this is discussed further in Chapter 10 (see page 151).

The Five Ps – Product

The consideration and planning required to improve an organisation's core activity – its products or services – is often thought of as self-evident, but that is to confuse selling with marketing. Sales is essentially about getting today's products and services to those people who are willing to buy or, more usually with charities, to those who most need the services being offered. Marketing can be perceived as 'selling tomorrow's products'. This at least has the merit of allowing the question 'how should tomorrow's products and services be different?' and by analogy 'should we be catering for different audiences?' In the planning process it is crucial to pose these questions. For fundraisers who are charged with this process it is vital to involve the operational part of the charity so that the main services of the organisation are considered as part of the marketing mix, not just the fundraising products and services. The results of external market research should play an important part in the analysis, and what competitors and other organisations are offering and planning to offer should be considered carefully. Equally, market research can help to identify areas and audiences that are not served by existing offerings or those which require slightly different products or services from those currently on offer.

The Five Ps – Price

When considering the price of products or services, a very careful assessment of what is offered by competitors against the organisation's market share (or at least its market position) is needed. For service-providing charities such as Leonard Cheshire, contracting with local authorities to provide care at home and residential services for disabled people, there are two distinct components:

1.   What the customer will pay (and in this case local authorities are notoriously price-sensitive).

2.   What the competition is charging (and there always is competition but it is perhaps not always apparent).

Leonard Cheshire Disability, for example, built a very detailed pricing and costing model that showed exactly what it costs to provide a week's residential care for any particular level of impairment. Frequently this is significantly higher than the price that local authorities have previously been willing to pay.

Through detailed negotiations, complete transparency and comparisons with valid like-for-like competition, the charity has been able to achieve very significant increases in the provision of existing care, albeit sometimes phased over two or three years. It is important to note that this does not take into account compliance with the Care Standards Act 2000 (enacted in April 2002) which, in effect, requires suppliers, not-for-profit and for-profit, to offer a new product (with a consequent increase in costs). That is, a level of residential care that must comply with specific, detailed criteria such as room sizes and levels of staffing that were not formerly recognised.

In consumer markets it is vital to understand the 'elasticity of demand' (Thirkettle 1970) Within many inelastic markets, because competition is so fierce, small increases in price, say for cornflakes, may lead to significant shifts in demand as consumers switch their buying patterns, even away from the market leader. In other elastic markets a price rise may have little effect on demand. Interestingly, this can be seen in the humble charity shop or on a bookstall in a jumble sale. To cite a personal example, the author changed the price of second-hand paperbacks on a charity bookstall from 20p to 40p each. The result was that demand did not change at all while monetary turnover (and profitability) doubled. Buyers either wanted a particular title or not, and having found it were certainly prepared to spend 40p on acquiring it. At subsequent sales an interesting experiment would have been to go on raising the price until demand began to fall and then revert to the one delivering maximum returns.

The Five Ps – Promotion

Many see promotion simply as the provenance of advertising but this part of the marketing mix goes so much further. Branding and the building of brand values are achieved largely through the use of an effective communication programme, having first ensured that the product is right. Promotion covers all aspects of advertising, use of media and media coverage, public relations, internal and external communications, customer/client relations, after-sales service and much more. An integrated plan is required, one which ensures that all channels through which news and information can reach customers and users are addressed and that a suitable programme is built and delivered to meet the required level of exposure.

'Orange' is a particularly good commercial example of a complete brand being built, principally through advertising promotion. Early advertisements showed no product, merely a concept, 'the future's bright, the future's Orange.' In just six words the advertisers were able to propose an optimistic statement with which most would want to agree and then use repetition to inculcate the brand name – a colour and a fruit liked by the vast majority of the population. Much editorial comment followed and by the time the actual product started appearing everyone was familiar with, and generally well disposed towards, the brand and the values espoused. Promotion continues through the whole communications process – sales incentives and display activities all the way to customer care and after-sales service – to ensure that the messages stay consistent and users remain satisfied with their investment. This was an excellent piece of marketing in that access to mobile phone technology had, in effect, become a commodity where, usually, price is king. Orange did not need to resort to discounting.

Case study: NSPCC

The NSPCC also used the full range of promotional tools in building and launching the Full Stop campaign. For a charity to commit itself very publicly to ending child cruelty was a brave (and some might say foolhardy) thing to do. Yet in reality it is only a restatement of the organisation's vision and mission: a clear, unequivocal, public restatement but a big, bold idea that does capture the imagination.

As Giles Pegram CBE, the organisation's long-time director of appeals, said: 'The advertising communication programme that followed the launch succeeded in reaching many people previously sympathetic to the charity but previously sufficiently unmoved to have actively supported them. Whilst the appeal target of £250 million was not reached within the original time frames, by extending the time frames the NSPCC raised £274 million, and increased its normal income from £50 million a year to £140 million a year.' The NSPCC itself remained convinced that it was the right campaign at the right time. Pegram, now a consultant, has said on many occasions that 'a successful major appeal not only raises a significant amount of money, it also transforms the organisation and its capacity for raising sustained income. The Full Stop campaign also linked rather neatly into the government's own commitment to end child poverty which is one of the major causes of child abuse'.

The Five Ps – Place

'Place' covers the whole subject more properly defined as distribution. That is, how and where customer need is met. For example, with a Leonard Cheshire residential care home this may well be seen as a given, yet one that needs to change. Historically, many homes were sited where a convenient property existed, such as an old country house that was bequeathed to the charity or, in the case of Staunton Harold (situated in Derbyshire), rescued from demolition by dint of a government grant and direct pressure on the family owners. Unfortunately, such locations, though set in beautiful parks in rolling countryside, are no longer acceptable to the majority of people who, increasingly, would rather have their own front doors and easy access to community facilities such as shops, pubs and cinemas. The Care Standards Act enshrined this need for disabled people and the charity embarked upon an extensive modernisation/new-build programme.

Distribution for the retail industry is a science in its own right. Logistics covers the whole gamut of the supply of the right goods into the right outlets in the right quantities at the right time. Supermarkets depend upon just-in-time systems – a production strategy which aims to minimise inventory and storage costs, thereby increasing return on investment by delivering products immediately before they are to be used. Fundraisers who are charged with delivering income growth through trading subsidiaries and shop chains are learning the same skills in order to improve profitability and customer satisfaction.

Place is an important part of the marketing mix which is sometimes overlooked when the provision of services – such as information – is again taken for granted via existing channels such as information leaflets and helplines. However, as the enormous take-up and growth in Internet services has shown, change is always with us and is perhaps the only constant that should be factored into marketing plans. How an organisation delivers its services is as important as the physical 'where', and both can be contained within considerations of distribution.

Case study: SouthBank Mosaics

SouthBank Mosaics (SBM) is a social enterprise, based in the Crypt of St John's Church opposite Waterloo Station. It works very successfully with young offenders to provide opportunities for participants to learn how to design and construct large-format mosaic panels (see figure 3.7). Previously, these panels had been commissioned by or sold to local authorities to use as street furniture. Participants took great pride in seeing their handiwork on public display and vandalism was never a problem.

However, by 2010 the organisation was finding the reduced funding levels with local authorities were making it hard to place finished panels and sculptures and so looked for marketing help via a Knowledge Transfer Partnership with London South Bank University. This enabled the social enterprise to receive six days' consultancy market research at no cost to the organisation. This research led directly to new ideas around alternative 'Places' and possible markets through the consideration of other targets such as building specifiers. In turn this has allowed the organisation to clarify its marketing, improve its funding and expand its outreach.

SBM founder David Tootill said: 'The research partnership with LSBU enabled us to look at marketing ideas we had not time or expertise ourselves to organise and has provided a very helpful boost at a very difficult time.'

FIGURE 3.7 ONE OF SBM'S MORE CHALLENGING MOSAIC PANELS, 'GRANNY AND THE HOODY'

The Five Ps – Position

The preceding elements, product, promotion, price and place are usually considered in-depth within the analysis for a marketing strategy. However, it is helpful in any strategic plan to think of positioning in terms of both individual products and the organisation itself. An organisation needs to consider not only on what basis it will compete within a chosen market or segment of a market (for example, high-priced, low-volume Rolls Royce or low-priced, high-volume Ford Ka) but also how it will provide a strategic positioning response in terms of its core mission and objectives. For example, the NSPCC, in seeking to end child cruelty, has to be seen as credible, authoritative and very well-resourced because such an outcome will take a huge investment to achieve.

Ries and Trout (1989) claim that when considering the issue of position, organisations have three distinct alternatives to pursue. First, an organisation can build upon its current position to create a distinctive perception of the brand by customers and target audiences. Avis consistently used the 'we try harder' slogan to make a virtue out of being number two to Hertz in the car hire market. Second, having established the attributes that are most important to its chosen audiences, users, customers or supporters, the organisation can see if there are any unoccupied positions that are desirable in the audience's minds and, therefore, any viable opportunities or positions to take up. Drummond and Ensor (2001) quote the example of IDV Ltd which looked at traditional sweet dark sherries versus pale and light dry sherries and identified an opportunity for a light-coloured sweet sherry. It launched Croft Original at a time when there was no other competitor and it became the best-selling sherry brand in the UK.

Where there has been a change in consumer behaviour, in society's attitudes or perhaps even an error in the original position adopted, repositioning may be considered. Many companies and charities attempt to reposition themselves in response to changing circumstances or market developments but this is not an easy task to perform successfully. Babycham abandoned the famous deer and trademark green bottle in 1993 in an effort to appeal to a wider market including young men. However, by 1993 it had abandoned all the changes, reverting to the traditional marks and returning to an appeal to a predominantly female audience. Charities are currently investing a great deal in name changes and recent examples include: British Diabetic Association to Diabetes UK; Marriage Guidance Council to Relate; The Distressed Gentlefolk's Association to Elizabeth Finn Trust; and The Sue Ryder Foundation to Ryder Care, among many others. These changes were made partly in response to a perceived need to reposition themselves and to appeal to larger audiences. Where there is a very clear need to reposition, the investment necessitated by a name and logo change may be justified, but in many cases changes seem to be made for the sake of doing something different.

Interestingly, repositioning can work very effectively for fundraising products. Many charities are experiencing over-capacity and declining demand for overseas challenge events (Third Sector 2007) and the Brooke is no exception. However, in their case, anyone who visits a Brooke project, which offers free veterinary care to working horses, mules and donkeys in Egypt, Jordan, India, Pakistan and Afghanistan, tends to become a very loyal, long-term supporter and advocate of the charity. By moving visits away from the challenge element and concentrating on paid visits by supporters and their friends, a significant boost to the high-value giver programme has been engineered.

Stephen Pidgeon, consultant, and former chair and founder of the direct marketing agency Tangible, has closely observed the efforts and detailed analysis of some not-for-profit organisations' attempts to define or redefine their position. In a personal interview in 2002 he commented that there are some good examples of organisations which are simply aiming to clarify what they are about. For example, he cited the National Trust in Scotland which has built upon the very Scottishness of the organisation – 'the heart of the nation' – and clearly incorporated that idea into its fundraising propositions, hoping for an organic growth in uptake and responses. He also pointed to the Salvation Army which has, in a similar way, consistently revisited its total, non-judgemental love of humanity and reflected that in its fundraising and communications messages – interestingly without any overt reference to its deep Christian beliefs that love of humanity is a reflection of godly love. Pidgeon feels that it is all too easy to change with the best of intentions and get it wrong. For example, the Distressed Gentlefolk's Association change to Elizabeth Finn Trust (the name of the organisation's founder) was done with the best of intentions, but does anyone recognise that name? And, most importantly, will anyone equate that to an organisation that works very hard on behalf of older people?

Ansoff's matrix

The matrix shown in figure 3.8, probably the best known of Ansoff's work and first postulated in the 1960s, is particularly useful to bear in mind throughout the planning process in terms of current and future development.

Figure 3.8 ANSOFF'S MATRIX

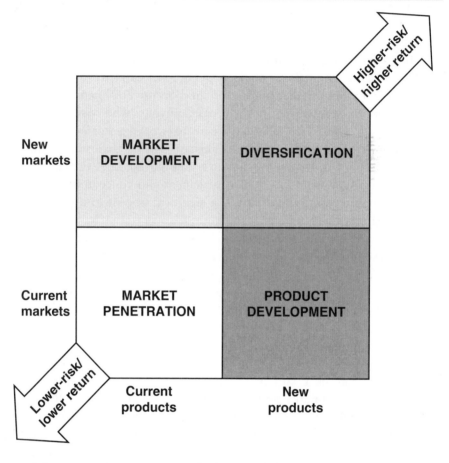

Most organisations start in the bottom left-hand corner of the matrix, thinking about their current products and services that are supplied to current customers or users. Marketing planning usually concentrates on development towards new markets or new services/products or both. Clearly either route involves risk but the highest risk with the greatest danger of failure is to move towards new markets with new products or services. Equally it is true that with sufficient planning and resources the greatest success in terms of growth may arise from such a manoeuvre.

The matrix can be used in a number of different ways. When Leonard Cheshire applied the matrix to their services back in 2002 it looked as illustrated in figure 3.9.

FIGURE 3.9 LEONARD CHESHIRE'S APPLICATION OF ANSOFF'S MATRIX

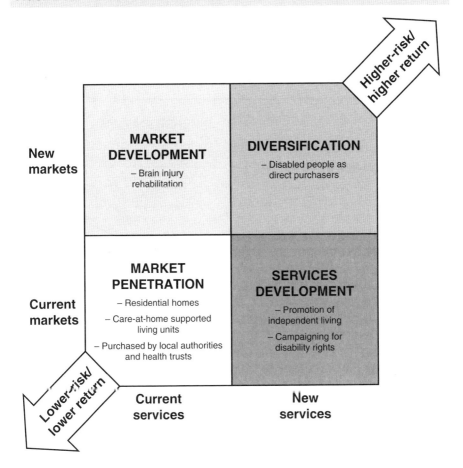

One of the major challenges for the organisation will be how to manage some of the transitions (especially in funding) that result as the mix of services begins to change over the next decade.

However, the matrix can also be used to help understand the current status (and possible future) of the fundraising product portfolio. With the example shown in figure 3.10 service purchasers, as opposed to voluntary income providers, have been excluded and the range simplified to illustrate the analysis more clearly.

A **product portfolio** is simply the range of products or product mix that an organisation offers. It may also be known as a product group. The issue that having a range of products creates is how to apportion investment in areas, such as promotion, across the portfolio. **Portfolio analysis** is the study of the product portfolio to decide what the optimum distribution of resources would be. This is done with the aim of improving performance in the market and increasing market share.

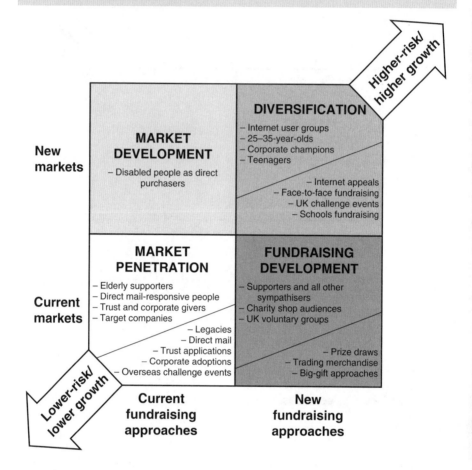

FIGURE 3.10 LEONARD CHESHIRE'S FUNDRAISING APPLICATION OF ANSOFF'S MATRIX

Thus, as can be seen in figure 3.10, legacies came from elderly supporters, while face-to-face canvassing was aimed at 25- to 35-year-old sympathisers. Direct mail was sent to those who were responsive to this medium, while prize draws (UK-wide draws were a new venture for the charity) were targeted at supporters and all other sympathisers. Approaches to trusts and companies are reasonably self-explanatory, though new approaches within target companies were aimed at persuading key decision-makers and influencers to become or persuade others to become internal champions for the charity. Similarly, the attempt to make Internet appeals work was aimed at specific groups within the total Internet user community. In the same way, trading was a new venture for the charity, which did not, historically, compete in the charity shop market or develop any coherent merchandising strategy. There were, therefore, both direct mail and Internet opportunities and, as the charity had overseas self-sufficiency projects, it was investigating the ethical marketing of products sourced from such projects. These were, however, higher risk than the placing of a new fundraising product to existing and new customers.

Overseas challenge events, which, as for many charities, were in decline, were being replaced by far more cost-effective UK-sponsorship events such as abseils and parachute jumps. Mass participation events such as the London marathon appealed to specific groups which, first and foremost, wanted to participate.

Another new activity for the organisation was specific approaches to wealthy individuals for major gifts. Income from UK voluntary groups such as Lions, Soroptomists, Round Table and Rotary were static but the schools market had yet to be tapped. With the increasing emphasis on materials that fitted the national curriculum there was an opportunity for the charity to develop and place suitable materials around disability equality issues as education and awareness vehicles. However, this was a high-risk investment in that the approach was for new products to new markets.

During the planning process one can go a step further with the analysis of existing fundraising products and chart them against the Boston Matrix.

The Boston Matrix

While this is probably one of the best-known models for portfolio analysis it is also one of the least understood. Developed by the Boston Consulting Group (BCC) in 1968, the work came out of the study of product life cycles. The standard matrix is concerned with the generation and use of cash within a business and can be used very effectively to analyse either a complete operation or business unit, or specific products and services. The two axes on the model represent relative market share and market growth.

On the one hand, relative market share is seen as a predictor of the ability to generate cash. This is based on the proposition that a high market share translates into a high volume of sales while investment in marketing and maintaining that position will be relatively smaller, if only through economies of scale. On the other hand, the potential for market growth is seen as a predictor of the need for cash investment in a product or service. Products in high-growth sectors require proportionately far higher investment to keep up with demand and the competition. Figure 3.11 illustrates the matrix.

FIGURE 3.11 THE BOSTON MATRIX

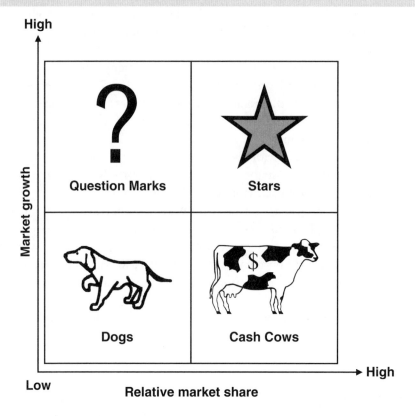

- 'Cash Cows' is the term used for products which enjoy a high market share in a relatively stable, mature market – thus they generate a positive cash flow.

- 'Stars' refer to (perhaps) newer products that enjoy a high profile in an expanding market. The investment necessary to maintain this position is high and therefore cash flow may be neutral or less positive.

- 'Question Marks' describe products in that sector where market share is low but the potential for growth remains high. Investment also, therefore, remains high and cash flow may well be negative.

- 'Dogs' (or even dead dogs) are seen as underperforming products in stable or declining markets with low or no growth and low relative market share. Cash flow is likely to be neutral or negative.

The great value of this analysis, when used accurately with the appropriate research, is that decisions can be made about products or services within the portfolio. Should Question Marks have further investment pumped in to turn them into Stars or should investment be cut right back to allow them to either die away or become a small Cash Cow, perhaps occupying a particular niche market? As growth falls and markets mature, should investment in Stars be frozen or cut back to milk them as Cash Cows? Should Dogs be put down, replaced or updated and relaunched as a niche product?

The matrix is predicated upon the parallel concept of product life cycles, also devised by the Boston Consulting Group, which has been described as the most quoted but least understood concept in marketing. The basic concept relates to four principal stages in the life of any product or service:

1. **introduction,** when investment is high;

2. **growth,** where investment continues and is even increased to ensure a high market share;

3. **maturity,** when the market stabilises and investment may be cut back; and

4. **decline,** when sales fall and decisions need to be made about an individual product's future.

These can be mapped against the four segments of the matrix to cross-check a product's actual position. It is of course vital to realise that an individual life cycle may last a season (as in fashion clothing), some years (as with cars) or even decades (as with many food and drink brands). Reinvestment, product or service innovation and repositioning can put an existing product into an entirely new cycle.

For fundraisers the axes can be changed to reflect more helpful indicators so as to plot the effectiveness of individual fundraising propositions and products. For example, an individual CSO might replace 'relative market share' with 'resourcing need' or 'return on investment', and 'market growth' with a realistic assessment of the 'potential growth'.

A further refinement may be to place each product within a circle denoting its relative contribution to the overall income. A simplified version for the Brooke Hospital for Animals might look like the illustration in figure 3.12.

FIGURE 3.12 BROOKE HOSPITAL FOR ANIMALS FUNDRAISING USE OF THE BOSTON MATRIX IN 2002

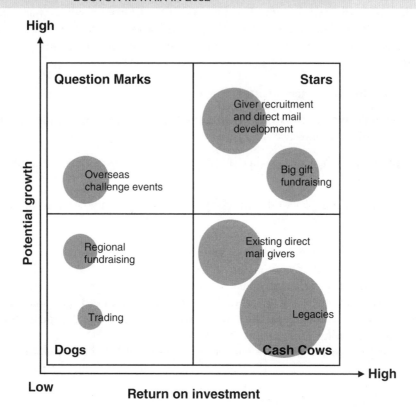

The matrix is highly adaptable to the individual needs of an organisation or sector, as figure 3.13 shows. This has been adapted from Montanari and Bracker by Drummond and Ensor (2001) and shows how a public sector portfolio can be drawn up by a campaigning charity.

FIGURE 3.13 A CAMPAIGNING APPLICATION OF THE BOSTON MATRIX

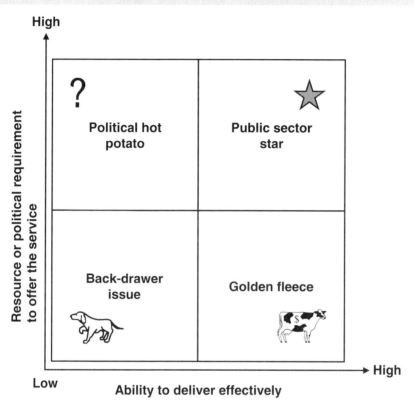

From this it should be possible to understand how issues could be mapped against the matrix to determine how best to apply scarce resources and effort.

Internal communications

As the whole of this chapter postulates, developing a marketing strategy needs to be part of a fully integrated process that is understood and agreed by the board and owned by the whole organisation. The most important audience for any marketeer is, in the view of Colin Mitchell (2002), the internal one. Mitchell asks, 'You tell your customers what makes you great but do your employees know?' He explains that internal marketing is so important because it is the best way to help employees (and, by extension, volunteers) to make a powerful emotional connection to the products and services that an organisation delivers. His view is that companies often ignore this critical constituency. He continues: 'Employees are unified and inspired by a common sense of purpose and identity. Unfortunately, in most companies internal marketing is done poorly, if at all.'

Mitchell argues fervently to link internal and external marketing so that staff understand and reinforce the messages that an organisation is trying to communicate to its chosen audience. Otherwise dissonance will interfere with otherwise powerfully orchestrated implementation plans and campaigns. When a beleaguered British Rail prematurely launched a campaign that announced service improvements under the title of 'we're getting there', they provoked extremely destructive press comment by drawing attention to the void between the promise and reality. As a result, staff who had been quite legitimately proud of real progress that had been made were thoroughly demoralised. Mitchell advocates a five-step approach to the creation of an internal communications strategy that will engage staff. The same approach may be valuable in gaining internal acceptance, understanding and assistance to implement a new marketing strategy.

• **Don't preach** – marketeers must draw on employee research to identify what staff are really thinking about, and ask rank-and-file staff to articulate the hopes, aspirations and vision.

• **Emphasise beliefs** – intentions are necessary but beliefs inspire and motivate people to care about the goals; intentions may change over time, the core beliefs should not.

• **Make the medium part of the message** – capture the attention and interest of the internal audiences by using surprise and intrigue. Rather than send out the same old memos and presentations, take risks and engage the audience (send a competition, for example).

• **Design materials to fit** – long tomes and manuals simply do not get read; IBM sent out a pamphlet parodying Chairman Mao's little red book, explaining why Linux was so important to the company's future, which was valued and actively used.

• **Have fun** – a cardinal rule for fundraising, it applies just as much to internal communications that usually are self-important and boring; humour, self-deprecation and genuine humility can achieve remarkable results in communicating a message and gaining its acceptance.

60-minute plans

When starting to think about marketing in an organisation, many people naturally start with the marketing strategy. It is possible and, as outlined, advisable for the marketing imperatives to drive overall strategy. It is common, however, that the strategic direction, some plans, if not a full strategic plan, and budgets will already be in existence before questions are asked as to how the funding and resources necessary to achieve the agreed objectives can be generated.

A strategic approach to the whole process takes a lot of time and needs to involve a very wide range of participants. However, if it is not possible for an organisation to go down the ideal recommended route, a start has to be made somewhere. If this is the case, much of the necessary work may already exist, albeit not in the form, detail and context required. Thus it is possible to draft a marketing strategy fairly quickly if very clear, achievable corporate objectives already exist. That part is crucial. If the required information and clarity exist, the process might then look something like this (see figure 3.14).

FIGURE 3.14 A SHORTENED MARKETING STRATEGY PLANNING CYCLE

While far from ideal, the rigour of this shortened process – and the need to communicate at every stage – will begin a journey during the course of which the organisation will come to understand what marketing, properly integrated and used, can achieve. The reality checks that the process imposes can be a very powerful aid to change and allow scope for far more detailed analysis and communication to proceed through to the next planning cycle. In the meantime, the 60-minute plan may be far more robust than targets and budgets that appear to be simply the chief executive's or chair's aspirations or, more usually for fundraisers, last year's results plus 5% or 10%.

Conclusion

In brief then, it is possible to plan a marketing strategy in an hour but it is far more effective to ensure understanding and ownership of the plans by the entire organisation. Integration starts with the board but needs to work top–down and bottom–up. A marketing strategy is probably the most important element of any comprehensive management plan, and its role in helping ensure successful implementation cannot be overstated.

Within any strategy it is, of course, vital that the planned objectives are spelled out clearly and unambiguously. For marketeers, who are seeking to communicate effectively with internal and external audiences, this is an imperative. One approach is to ensure that all objectives are made to be SMART. This does not imply that they are particularly clever or skilful, merely that they can be achieved and that everyone knows that has happened.

SMART objectives therefore are:

- **Specific** – for clarity, transparency and understanding;
- **Measurable** – to allow effective monitoring and reporting of successes and failures;
- **Aspirational** – high enough to challenge and inspire high effort; but also
- **Realistic** – targets must be achievable, otherwise people will quickly become uninterested and even demoralised;
- **Timescaled** with agreed milestones – to permit proper review and feedback.

However, a variation of the normal criteria might allow for greater creativity and ownership and it is important not to become too mechanistic. Many of the objectives and measures should be non-financial and relate to the performance of the organisation as a whole. CSOs in particular need to consider outcomes rather than outputs. That is, the impact their work has rather than the way they spend their money. Most of all, everything must contribute to the brand and should ensure coherence in preserving and building upon the reputation of the organisation, as will be seen in the next chapter.

CHAPTER FOUR

The charity as a brand

When I have finished, if a solution is not beautiful, I know it is wrong.
Buckminster Fuller

I cannot and will not cut my conscience to fit this year's fashions.
Lillian Hellman

Looking briefly at the origins and development of branding as a key element of the marketing mix, this chapter examines issues around brand values and how CSOs, in particular, use their reputations to promote the objectives and work of the organisation. Comparisons with commercial brands are made and key developments examined for indicators of success. Some useful examples of rebranding exercises are also examined and conclusions drawn.

Perspectives

Branding was originally about simple ownership. Egyptian brick-makers made a unique impression in the bricks they produced in order to identify their own bricks, and thus the quantity they had supplied to a site. In the USA cattle ranchers literally branded their animals by burning a unique mark, usually signifying the ranch name, into the hides of their cattle. This was done in order to identify them anywhere on the vast tracts of open range where they grazed, to deter casual rustlers and make it easier to distinguish between them at market. Farm animals and horses continue to be marked with a similar security brand, though today it may be an electronic tag.

The idea of an ownership mark that signifies quality or other distinct values came to the fore with the advent of advertising, when manufacturers started putting their name on their products to establish a competitive advantage over the offerings of others. At this point branding moved on from simply signifying ownership and began to represent the values and the qualities espoused by owners and manufacturers. This happened as the need to make use of an improved production capacity and a reliable nation-wide distribution network led manufacturers such as Cadbury and Dunlop to adopt mass advertising techniques. George and Richard Cadbury realised that they needed to stimulate demand for their products and began to promote values including goodness and wholesomeness to differentiate the chocolate from that of the competitors: the brand, as we know it, was born.

In 1870, Dr Thomas John Barnardo opened his first home for children in London's impoverished East End. He had been moved by the plight of large numbers of homeless children sleeping rough. Following the death of one boy that Barnardo turned away because the home was already overfull, he vowed 'never again'. His own name was used for the charity and he developed a strapline that was intended to make the values his charity espoused attention-grabbing: 'no child will ever be refused admission'. These words were painted in six-foot high letters over the gate of the home. Chapter 8 shows how Barnardo's today associates itself with 'shocking' images of suffering, which are designed to be impossible to ignore.

These examples demonstrate how a CSO's brand must reflect the qualities and values held by the organisation.

Brand identity

Having a strong brand identity is fundamentally important for a CSO because the public and others who deal with that organisation need to be able to recognise, trust and connect with this identity, understanding what the organisation does. It allows people to see clear differences between one CSO and another, the aim of this being that they will choose to lend their committed support to that organisation. The following examples show how charity brands have been developed and protected over the years.

WWF has spent many years developing its brand identity in order to clarify and emphasise the role of the organisation in environmental concerns, rather than that of preserving threatened wildlife. As part of this new identity, it changed its name from the World Wildlife Fund to the World Wide Fund for Nature, while continuing to promote the well-known WWF logo with its instantly recognisable Panda symbol. As Margaret Bennett (former director of fundraising at WWF) said in a personal interview in 2002 'There was great debate about the changes and some countries still have not fallen into line', despite the fact that the WWF brand name and panda trademark are worth a great deal. Commercial marketeers know this and are prepared to pay for their brands to be linked to the panda. Interestingly, WWF vigorously defended the abbreviation successfully against the World Wrestling Federation, which then changed its trading name to World Wrestling Entertainment (WWE 2002).

The global brand IBM had to reinvent itself in the personal computer market after losing out badly to software rival Microsoft (Rodgers 1986). International Business Machines, the world leader in mainframe computers in the 1970s, soon became an also-ran in the PC market of the 1980s, when the disk operating system was licensed by Microsoft to dozens of other manufacturers. Dell and Compaq, among others, sold far more PCs than IBM, which has subsequently revisited its roots and branded itself as *the* company to provide a complete answer to networking, systems and e-commerce. With this approach, it has enjoyed something of a resurgence.

Leonard Cheshire, like Barnardo's, another charity bearing its founder's name, has for some time been endeavouring to re-establish its brand. The charity is the UK's largest not-for-profit organisation working with disabled people, yet in 2010 it had a prompted awareness of under 50% of the adult population (nfpSynergy 2010). From the 1960s to the 1980s the Leonard Cheshire Foundation benefited enormously from Cheshire's own celebrity status as a highly decorated Second World War hero and flying ace. Cheshire would write full-page emotive articles in the national press, appear on television, radio and cinema and open new homes, often visiting exotic faraway places. Cheshire was a charismatic figure and had a widespread public appeal. The charity attracted gifts, both large and small, from admirers who had been touched by his words and work.

Yet following Cheshire's death in 1992, the charity quickly realised that it had not built upon that celebrity status to establish a brand that could survive without its founder. There was no database of givers and knowledge of wealthy friends and favourably disposed trusts was at best in people's heads and at worst died with Cheshire. In 2001, while 80% of men over the age of 60 could recognise the charity's name, awareness among the under-35s had dropped to less than 20% (author-commissioned research 2001).

Adopting the disabled-parking orange badge for its Enabled campaign, Leonard Cheshire brought greater awareness to the issues of disability, but did little to link this to its own master brand, to the extent that few people realised that Enabled was owned by the charity. The presentation of the brand was too fragmented. Later advertising sought to address this issue and reconnect the sub-brand of Enabled as an important part of Leonard Cheshire's work, with advertising targeted at younger age groups to strengthen this refocus. Consequently, all above- and below-the-line marketing reflected the same issues, images and messages of 'enabling ordinary lives'. In 2006 there was a loud outcry at suggestions that the name might be changed completely and so instead the charity formally added Disability to its name in July 2007, trading as Leonard Cheshire Disability. The organisation seeks to regain ground lost to other organisations dealing with the issues surrounding disability policy and practice.

The charity that was set up after the death of Diana Spencer made its own branding mistakes. The Memorial Fund was set up after Princess Diana's death in 1997. In the wake of the enormous surge of public sympathy (and some would say morbid curiosity) the fund was able to gain 'ownership' of the Diana brand, adopting the Princess's signature as its logo. However, some of its early decisions on how to market the brand, particularly allowing Flora margarine to feature the signature logo due to the charity's association with the London Marathon, met with a public and media backlash. More prudent decisions have been made since, and in its first three years, the Fund made £35 million of grants with £100 million of assets (DPWMF 2000). But, as with many endowment funds, it risked a gradual decline from public view as a new generation who never knew Diana replaces the one so deeply moved. Very interestingly, the trustees finally agreed in 2007 that the trust would become time limited and work to give the entire endowment away by 2012 (DPWMF 2012). That at least avoids questions about the longevity of the name and support.

Even for a cause that is well known by the British public, branding work is seen as necessary. The Samaritans (founded by Chad Varah) rebranded in 2002 for the first time in its 60-year history, with the aim of increasing donations and volunteer numbers. The charity's market research found that while a large proportion of the public – 90% – was aware of its existence, not many of those surveyed could describe its services accurately. While the organisation provides support to anyone who needs it – not only those who are suicidal – the people surveyed commonly said that they understood the service only to be for suicidal people. It therefore attempted to reposition itself to improve public understanding of its larger role. The Samaritans' volunteers, who are the key service deliverers, were fully briefed about the rebranding, which was developed by consultancy Wolff Olins. It included poster and press campaigns and simplifying the charity's name to 'Samaritans' (Prasad 2002).

Simon Armson, then the charity's chief executive, said in a personal interview (2002) 'There is a perception that people's problems have to be extreme before they contact a Samaritan. We're making it clear that suicide reduction remains very central to our philosophy but that people may not be actively suicidal to need help and support.' He added: 'Samaritans is to do with coping and finding a way forward. That's what we've always been.' The rebranding also aimed to expand the organisation's supporter base. Armson continued: 'I hope that more people will want to donate to us and see that we are relevant. If they can see the organisation more clearly in its context, then hopefully it will be more attractive to them.'

Unpacking brand identity

One helpful way of looking at this brand identity is to examine the 'three Ps of branding'; that is, Personality, Physique, and Presentation. It is useful when developing or implementing a brand strategy to analyse how the brand itself is perceived, in terms of its personality and physical attributes, and then how it is observed through its presentation in all guises. Figure 4.1 illustrates the relationships. Any dissonance will reflect badly upon the brand, creating confusion among potential customers and dissatisfaction among users.

A **brand strategy** is a long-term plan for the brand and the marketing support needed for it. It includes determining target audiences, their characteristics and understanding their preferences, expectations and what they need to know about the brand. It outlines the steps that the brand needs to take to create the support needed to create and sustain a successful CSO.

Figure 4.1 ELEMENTS OF BRAND IDENTITY

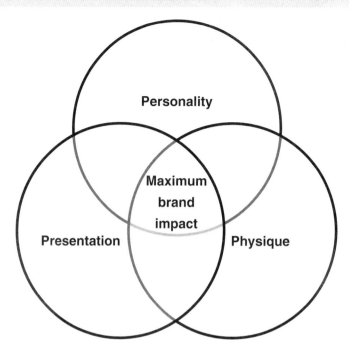

Brand personality

Brand personality (the very essence and soul of the proposition) should reflect the qualities and values espoused. In this way, Nike has used Michael Jordan very effectively over a long period to endorse and reflect the brand's youthful, virile, athletic, challenging and successful portrayal of life (as long as you wear the right trainers). In fact Jordan is now a sub-brand within an enlarged Nike organisation. On the other hand, Tiger Woods' sponsors dropped him very quickly after the debacle in 2009 (involving an extra-marital affair) rather than risk reputational damage by continuing with his endorsements.

The use, therefore, of celebrity endorsement by charities crucially must fit with the organisation's existing values while avoiding conflict with planned programmes and possible changes. Only then can the CSO seek meaningful sponsorship with corporate organisations. There must be a good match with either the celebrity's own persona or the company, one that offers a convincing fit between the celebrity's or the commercial brand's values and those of the CSO. Where such suitable partners are found, a strong match can be established and a long-lasting, mutually beneficial relationship will result.

Brand physique

Brand physique (sometimes referred to as the tone of voice or the very feel of the offering) embraces the physical attributes of a product or organisation. For example, the United Colours of Benetton chose to portray itself as aggressive and challenging in its above-the-line advertising. Many of the images used by Benetton were certainly shocking, but in the longer term this did not prove successful in helping to sell expensive clothing. The brand, however, is still seen to be somewhat controversial, different and challenging. Perhaps another more tangible manifestation of physique is that of the tone of voice: how the brand speaks to the customer or recipient of any particular communication. Thus most people perceive Coca-Cola as youthful, energetic, positive and well-intentioned because of the tone, style and nature of the communications that the company puts out. Coke owns the imagery, the song, the bottle shape and the youthful energy. Similarly the RNLI is perceived as robust, reliable, always there in an emergency, strong, rugged and dependable. Everything that it does reinforces that perception and delivers a particular tone or physical presence to its various audiences.

Brand presentation

Brand presentation (the outside appearance), the way packaging, advertising and promotion represents the brand to the public, is perhaps the most visible of the three Ps. Retail outlets clearly need to convey the values espoused by their parent organisation, hence the appearance and even feeling inside a Tesco store is very different from that in a branch of Marks & Spencer. Intel owns the four-note signature which was launched as part of the Intel Inside campaign and, thanks to being a jingle, is recognisable even on the radio. Charity shops similarly need to reflect the charity's brand values accurately. Sue Ryder shops demonstrate the thrift, economy and compassion espoused by their founder, and a move up-market would endanger the brand perception of shop volunteers and customers alike. On the other hand, Oxfam's specialisation into books and furniture in some of its shops fits more comfortably with the educational and developmental aspirations and values of the charity. Likewise the representation of some Oxfam specialist outlets to retail more designer brands and fashionable items, at higher prices, reinforces the organisation's lead in charity retail and customers' ability to make valuable finds for themselves – whatever their particular needs are.

A good example of the way in which this analysis has been used is with the work that Arthritis Care conducted in developing its brand identity during the 1990s. As discussed in Chapter 2, in 1983 the charity changed its name (from the British Rheumatism and Arthritis Association) in order to reflect more accurately its caring and supportive work, and to differentiate the charity from Arthritis Research Campaign (arc), the only other national arthritis charity and one which funds *only* research (and is now called Arthritis Research UK). Throughout the 1990s, however, the organisation worked hard at improving user involvement to become an organisation 'of' disabled people rather than 'for' them. By 1999 the board of trustees had a majority of people with personal experience of arthritis as members. The new name was retained but the strapline in 1998 became 'empowering people with arthritis'. To quote Richard Gutch (chief executive 1992–2001) from a personal interview in 2002, 'The *care* in the name had changed from *caring for* people with arthritis to *caring about* the issues that concern people with arthritis'. The refocus was and still is reflected in all the organisation's communications, publications, policy work and promotion, both internal and external.

The power of brand values

Charities generally have distinct advantages when it comes to developing and communicating brand values. Changing the world is a pretty big idea. Whether it is Friends of the Earth, which set out to save the planet, or the Donkey Sanctuary, which set out to protect donkeys from cruelty and enable them to have a happy old age, ideas and values can be readily identified. In each case programmes are developed to communicate these effectively to the organisation's chosen audiences.

Case study: Oxfam

The Oxford Committee for Famine Relief was set up in 1942 as one of a number of groups in the UK aiming to highlight the problems created by the Nazi occupation of Greece, requesting that relief be sent to those in most urgent need. In 1943 the Oxford Committee for Famine Relief was registered as a charity and its first appeal – Greek Week – raised £12,700 for the Greek Red Cross. This was a remarkable achievement if you bear in mind that the brand was unknown, and people in war-torn Britain, who were already undergoing rationing, were then being asked to give funds to combat hunger in a far-away theatre of the war.

Since then Oxfam has consistently pioneered advertising and promotional methods, later adopted by other charities and the commercial world alike. Its modern name, taken from the telex abbreviation of its longer name, was formally adopted in 1965, by which time the brand was widely recognised as being authoritative, reliable, and able to move quickly and effectively. During the 1960s and 1970s, through the great work of Harold Sumption, considered by many to be the father of modern fundraising, Oxfam's brand values were presented graphically through simple advertisements and direct mail. These used courier fonts to appear type-written and urgent while simultaneously tapping into the public's conscience and goodwill. Oxfam is still one of a minority of CSOs to have taken the integration of its communications seriously. A consistent feel is present throughout its publications, print, Internet and advertising, though fully integrating marketing into an organisation is a very long journey.

For-profit organisations have long understood the need to communicate consistent brand values and this is clearly seen in the example provided by Scottish Widows. Financial service marketing has many similarities to the marketing of many charities in that the services offered are intangible, often not actively sought and rarely fully understood by customers. Despite this, the use of the Scottish Widow (literally the image and use of a young attractive female figure dressed in a long black cloak) for several years in all advertising, sales promotion, publications and other marketing materials has created a sense of trust within the public's mind second to none, according to Jeremy Prescot, now partner at Twentyone Twelve Communications (personal communication 2010). He said:

> As financial service companies go, Scottish Widows has established a clarity and confidence that speaks volumes for keeping the messages simple. Too many not-for-profit organisations still haven't understood the value of the brands they own and the need to communicate simple, consistent messages to the public in order to create firstly awareness, secondly understanding and then, and only then, empathy with the cause.

This is very reminiscent of the sales mnemonic **AIDA** which very usefully reminds us that it is essential, within any sales cycle, to create:

- Attention;

- Interest;

- Desire; and

- Action.

The many attempts to shorten or short circuit this cycle may have occasional success but will rarely provide sustained activity over the longer term. The acronym is a very useful one for any communicators to use to remind themselves that proper communication and understanding is a process that can rarely be reduced to a single message or campaign.

Creating ownership of the brand

While, as Oxfam illustrates, brand values can be one of the most powerful elements in modern charity marketing, unless they are lived and realised daily by those individuals who work within or support an organisation, those very values are empty and worthless. Ownership is the key to realising the power of a brand and charities must work as hard as commercial organisations to achieve buy-in of brand values at all levels.

As with those companies in service industries where staff meet or deal with customers every day, so it is the volunteers and staff within charities, those who work at the real grass roots, who are positioned to hold the greatest brand equity. In fact, charities should bring a variety of stakeholders into establishing their brand if the process is to be a success. This includes not only staff and active volunteers but also senior volunteers such as trustees, givers and service-users or beneficiaries who must also be consulted. Every individual attached to an organisation has a particular perspective on the brand values that they perceive and that have attracted them to support a particular cause.

One useful exercise in developing a brand and its inherent values is to bring a cross-section of these stakeholders together, inviting representatives from each group on the strength of their ability to champion the eventually emerging brand among their peers and colleagues. Once brought together in this way, stakeholders can be asked to share their views on the organisation, with questions that encourage creative expression, such as 'if the organisation were an animal, what sort of animal would it be?' While that type of question may sound frivolous, it will get people talking and should reveal valuable insights into how individuals view a particular cause, allowing participants to express their emotional response to an organisation in a tangible way that can be readily understood.

If holding a meeting of stakeholders or a series of smaller focus groups is not feasible, or the views of a much larger group of individuals are required, then paper and online surveys can prove a useful alternative. A questionnaire can be mailed to as many people as the budget permits, provided sufficient resources are available to collate and analyse the responses when they come back. Online surveys have distinct cost, distribution and analysis advantages. The drawback of either, however, is that some participants will perceive it as remote and impersonal, and are more likely to suggest that an organisation is simply paying lip service to involving individuals in the development of a brand. For this reason, care must be taken in constructing the questions of a survey and it must be made clear at the outset what weight and influence respondents will have within the overall process. For example, leading questions must be avoided and a route to respond appropriately to criticisms and comments must be given so that participants feel empowered rather than led or pushed into answers.

Whatever methods are used to involve stakeholders, it is unlikely that the brand values that emerge will be totally alien or unexpected to anybody. Brands are a distillation of the attitudes, perceptions and values that come from within an organisation, and anyone who works for or supports a particular cause should have some empathy with those attitudes and values. Of course, in the charitable context, a brand also has to be consistent with the established legal objects of the respective organisation. Changed brand values that appear imposed from outside without a clear rationale will not only seem alien to stakeholders, who might reject any sense of ownership, but also those values are likely to be intrinsically at odds with what stakeholders perceive or understand to be the core charity values.

Achieving internal ownership of the brand

Once the brand has been developed through consultation, part of the process of achieving wider ownership of the brand involves effective internal communication throughout the charity. As stated earlier, those individuals involved at the start of the process, when the brand values have been distilled, should be urged and expected to serve as brand champions within their stakeholder groups. In this way, a respected and well-connected volunteer – who has helped to define a charity's brand – can then use their own personal and professional networks to explain how those values have been arrived at, what the brand stands for and how other volunteers can help to communicate the values and messages to others.

This type of approach will be much more successful than an edict from the senior management team, or trustee body, that simply states 'this is our brand' and expects everyone immediately to buy into the end product. A more likely result of the latter approach will be to disenfranchise vast numbers of people from the entire brand development process; they will never believe, and therefore never communicate, the brand values in their work. Internal communication vehicles such as newsletters, team briefings and even conferences can be used to reinforce brand values, ideally calling on examples of how the brand is being realised at various levels of the charity. However, this must not be seen as a replacement for more personal communication and endorsement. Above all, it is critically important that trustees and any senior management team members sign up to the brand at the outset and are seen publicly to espouse and fulfil the brand values. Too many senior figures in charities pay scant regard to their brand, believing it has little to do with their concerns, which may rest in operations, resources or finance. However, this lack of engagement is very quickly detected by staff and volunteers who may themselves be sceptical of the brand development process and its outcomes. The absence of endorsement from the top of any organisation usually signals the failure of an initiative and never more so than when establishing or reinforcing a brand that must run through every level of a charity to be successful.

Diversification: a step too far?

Having established a strong and clearly defined brand, it is then a logical next step for some organisations to extend that brand into other areas and markets, reaching more and wider audiences. Such a move should, of course, be consistent with the marketing strategy. Too many charities, and their commercial counterparts, see market share as an end in itself. It is not, and if a charity's strategy clearly identifies a single, highly targeted audience, it can be wasting time, money and other valuable resources in taking its brand elsewhere, at least until it has achieved the aims of its original strategy.

If a charity's marketing strategy does allow or requires the extension of its brand, there are several ways in which this may be pursued. One increasingly popular commercial model is the transference of established brands into areas of operation with which they have not previously been associated. Perhaps the most prevalent of these areas is in financial services, where some of the strongest retailing brands – from Tesco to Marks & Spencer – have attempted to sell banking and investment products to existing and new customers. This is not always successful – just because there is potential synergy between having a desire to purchase and the capacity to purchase, this does not mean that all companies will necessarily succeed at the marketing of financial products. Indeed, some are already withdrawing from the market, acknowledging that they have little experience in offering financial services and that their customers do not necessarily see their familiar brands as belonging in this field.

When it comes to successful transference and diversification of a brand, there can be few examples, in the UK or indeed anywhere, greater than that of Virgin. Originally established as a record label in the early 1970s, the Virgin brand has been extended into a dizzying number of markets, from soft drinks and clothing manufacture to airline and rail operations, and now even financial services and mobile communications. Through all of these markets the figure of Richard Branson has loomed large, for within Virgin Branson is seen as the epitome of the company's brand values, standing for trust, entrepreneurship and innovation. It is perhaps too early to say if Virgin's aggressive forays into new markets have been an overall success or failure and some have already been divested. Certainly there have been notable problems, perhaps the greatest being in the case of Virgin Trains. Here the brand was applied to an existing service over which Virgin had little real influence beyond surface decoration and window dressing. Virgin's brand values of entrepreneurship, innovation and reliability have, therefore, experienced an uncomfortable ride.

Few charities have attempted brand diversification on this scale. One example that does stand out is Charity Projects with its Comic Relief brand. In fact, it might be argued that here the charity has achieved far greater success with its Red Nose activities than its commercial counterparts have managed. Clothing, music, books and fashion accessories have all conveyed the Comic Relief brand and managed to remain consistent with the values of the main biennial fundraiser, providing fun in a socially responsible manner. Breakthrough Breast Cancer has also achieved similar success, if on a smaller scale, with its own forays into clothing, music and fashion events. The 'fit' has been deemed apposite and accepted by the consumer.

There are other routes to diversification that have proved more attractive in recent years, often due to their accessibility and low financial risk to the charity. Cause-related marketing, from event sponsorship through to elaborate Charity of the Year schemes, has involved companies and CSOs in many high-profile brand marriages, intending to boost sales for the company and attract new supporters for the charity. While there have been some highly successful fits – for example, Tesco and its Computers for Schools initiative and Walkers with the similarly branded Books for Schools – the public has not always seen the logic behind these relationships. An example of the problem of brand discord can be found in HelpAd, an initiative of the International Red Cross Movement in the 1990s. This was a highly ambitious scheme which involved the brokering of partnerships between mutually beneficial brands such as Hovis and Marmite. Manufacturers would join in on-pack promotions, donating the monetary value of this advertising to the Red Cross Movement. But beyond the companies involved, there was no real brand synergy that aligned these manufacturers and their highly commercial products with the care services and international aid provided by the Red Cross. Unsurprisingly, the public failed to take the promotion to its heart, and the scheme was quietly dropped.

Similar cases of brand dissonance can be found in the commercial sector. Pret A Manger is a recent example, a brand synonymous with quality food that is aimed at an informed, professional consumer. The founders Julian Metcalfe and Sinclair Beecham continue to be significant shareholders. There was, however, hostility from both the media and the public when the company sold a minority shareholding to McDonald's, a brand tarnished over many years by allegations over its manufacturing processes. The deal was doubtless struck on financial grounds, providing Pret with extra capital investment. Interestingly, the majority stake in the company was acquired by European equity firm Bridgepoint in 2008, buying out McDonald's minority share (Attwood 2008). Although this change passed by largely unnoticed, any longer-term damage to Pret's brand equity has been avoided through the removal of McDonald's as a shareholder.

There are other avenues to brand extension and development that can prove less contentious. Partnerships behind the Children's Promise (a consortium of children's charities) and Will Aid (a consortium of international aid charities) along with recent high-profile mergers such as that of Terrence Higgins Trust and the London Lighthouse, mark another emerging trend in the sector. Again, the rationale behind these initiatives is doubtless sound – minimising or cutting back on expenditure while hopefully maximising the fundraising potential of such partnerships – but the effect on the brand values and loyalty of participating charities should not be underestimated. The Children's Promise may have encouraged Britain's workforce to donate an hour's salary to 'children's charities', but how many individuals taking part engaged directly with the specific brands of participating charities? The likes of the NSPCC and Barnardo's have spent many years attempting to differentiate their work and their brand values in the eyes of the public. Activities such as the Children's Promise would have done little to support that effort beyond creating some short-term effect on the organisation's bottom line.

The lesson here, in all these examples, is for charities to apply just as rigorous an analysis to any new markets and marketing initiatives as they have to those in which they traditionally operate. Once a robust marketing strategy and a clear brand identity have been established and bought into at all levels of an organisation, they should not be ignored at the first sign of a potentially large cheque. Any proposal to associate with third-party brands must be evaluated to see if the respective brand values match. Without this, the risk of brand dissonance and often public failure is too great for charities reasonably to take.

Brand recognition and loyalty

According to a *Marketing* magazine survey, both Cancer Research UK and Macmillan Cancer Support are in the top 50 loved brands in the country (Clark 2008), beating global brands such as YouTube, Manchester United and Levi's which spend tens of millions of pounds each year to advertise and promote their corporate brands. These findings tally with the Charity Brand Index, which placed Macmillan Cancer Support in the top spot and Cancer Research in second place in a prompted awareness survey, and vice versa in 2012 (Third Sector Research 2009, 2012). Furthermore, nfpSynergy's Charity Awareness Monitor (a regular tracking survey of the public's knowledge, understanding, attitudes and awareness of charities, including spontaneous and prompted awareness among the public in the UK) placed Cancer Research UK at number one in the top ten charities that first come to people's minds (i.e. spontaneous awareness), Macmillan at number eight, and the RSPCA and the NSPCC second and third, in that order (nfpSynergy 2009).

Case study: Great Ormond Street Hospital (GOSH)

As Marion Allford (1993) explains, the successful Great Ormond Street Wishing Well Appeal, launched in 1987, is a useful example of how a major capital appeal can also be used as a brand-building device. GOSH was already probably one of the best known hospitals in London, if not in the UK. Following the successful appeal, which raised £54 million (£12 million ahead of its target), the hospital is now certainly the best known (excluding perhaps Holby General in the BBC television soap *Casualty*). The key lesson one can learn from this is that the meticulous three years of planning included very careful analysis of the brand's strengths and weaknesses, and built upon these attributes to persuade all sections of society to buy into the importance and urgency of helping GOSH.

In 2011, the fundraising team was still receiving many unsolicited gifts and offers of fundraising activities because people believe in the brand and the value of offering help. This has helped enormously with the planning and implementation of a further campaign to complete the redevelopment programme.

Recognition, however, certainly does not guarantee loyalty. French Connection in the UK ran its controversial FCUK advertising campaign for some years. Like Benetton before it, it achieved huge media coverage, comment and awareness. The question remained, however, as to whether French Connection really did much to add value to its brand and gain increased loyalty from its customers. The dissonance between the 'in your face', irreverent campaign and the experience of shopping in an FCUK store was considerable and the campaign hasn't been used since 2007.

In commercial marketing, customer loyalty to the brand is crucial where a premium is sought and where repeat purchases are vital to sales growth and profitability. For charities, brand loyalty, where a person continues to give to one specific charity within a particular category (such as international aid) rather than to a number which all appear similar, is something different. Givers have favourite causes and users often become givers themselves, particularly at the end of their lives through a legacy. Why would anybody write a charity into their will – unless perhaps to annoy or spite the family – without a sense of loyalty to that charity's brand? Customer care is clearly very relevant, but how does the charity brand gain loyalty?

An analysis of behavioural drivers, using an onion construct (see figure 4.2), may be helpful in this context (adapted from Fishbein and

Ajzen 1975). On the outside is behaviour: how we act or react to a given stimulus. Underneath are our attitudes, which clearly have an effect on our behaviour. Under those attitudes lie our beliefs: the things we hold to be true or at least have faith in. Thus while one can change behaviour through superficial stimulation and persuade someone to buy (or give), it is more effective to obtain a change of attitude which will then impact behaviour more radically. Better still is to address the innermost beliefs. This is, of course, the hardest, which is why the Jesuits said 'Give me the child until six and I'll give you the man'. However, without at least gaining a resonance within an individual's belief structure, any support will, at best, be transitory and subject to change.

FIGURE 4.2 A MODEL ILLUSTRATING THE RELATIONSHIP BETWEEN HUMAN BEHAVIOUR AND BELIEFS

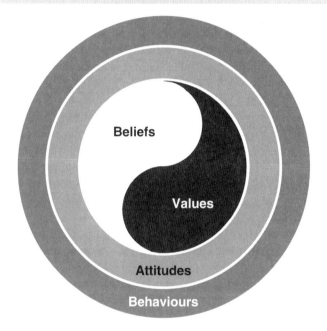

We see this in peer pressure, particularly among younger consumers; *Cabbage Patch Dolls* gave way to *Teenage Mutant Ninja Turtles* who themselves then fell before the might of the *Teletubbies* followed by the *Toy Story* characters, and so on. Adult behaviours are little different. It may be important perhaps to be seen at the Macmillan Ball, but unless those supporters actually share the values espoused by the organisation – its vision and mission – it is unlikely that they would ever do more than buy tickets to the next event. This may be fine in the short term but is unlikely to produce the impetus to write that charity into those supporters' wills.

Conveying the brand through corporate identity

Brands may be manifested in many ways – through customer experiences, through product development, through advertising – but one of the most effective ways to convey a brand is through a strong corporate identity. Brand identity is referred to as a corporate identity when talking about an organisation as a whole – how it is viewed and would like to be viewed by others, rather than the organisation's products and services. Corporate identity can provide a shortcut to brand values that can transcend languages, religions and international boundaries. A survey by Edelman Public Relations showed that in 2003 the top two most trusted brands in Europe, as ranked by trust from a mix of corporate and NGO brands, were the global NGO brands Amnesty International and WWF (Quelch and Laidler-Kylander 2006). Just as anywhere in the world Coca-Cola can be relied upon for refreshment and McDonald's for cheap fast food, the WWF represents clear and understandable values about its care for endangered species and Amnesty International for its human rights campaigning. Each of these super-brands also possesses a distinctive and widely recognised logo, utilising shape, characters and colours. The number of people around the world who do not recognise the golden arches of McDonald's is surely falling rapidly.

Corporate identity is often misinterpreted simply to mean an organisation's logo. Certainly, logos are an important component of any identity but they are just one of many elements, the most basic of which also include colour, typestyles and straplines. For example, the corporate identity of the British Red Cross is the distinctive red cross on a clear white background; the use of a carefully selected red (Pantone 032), white and black as a minimum in all publications and marketing, including its website; and the typefaces Bembo and Helvetica. With these few simple elements, a distinct identity can be extended through internal documents, external advertising and posters, fundraising brochures, clothing and vehicles, all providing points of consistency, whatever the variance in messages and audience.

However, corporate identity extends beyond such simple signifiers. It is also embodied in how an organisation presents itself in words and images. The style of any communication says just as much about an organisation. Images can be used to highlight the positive aspects of a cause, portraying beneficiaries with respect as individuals who have control over their lives. Alternatively, some charities trade on images of despair and of desperate need. Both approaches may be valid for certain organisations but each will influence the way in which individuals perceive and interact with the brand. So too can a choice of words. For example, Leonard Cheshire Disability ensures that the language in its marketing and communications protects the dignity of its service users. It does not talk about the disabled, an amorphous group which needs help, but rather refers constantly to disabled people as individuals who face challenges in society and to whom the charity offers constructive help.

As has been stated earlier, implementing brands effectively is critical if the values and equity in those brands are to be maintained. Many large companies are fortunate in having dedicated marketing departments and professionals at all levels and locations within an organisation which can maintain certain standards in how the brand is projected.

In CSOs such resources are rarely, if ever, available. Brands are constantly interpreted and conveyed by staff and volunteers whose day-to-day job is delivering direct charitable services and volunteers are often not constrained by conventional management channels. Regulating the use of a brand in these circumstances can be very difficult, if not impossible. Marketing materials might be produced by dozens of individuals to varying standards. The best solution is, usually, to be as supportive as possible. If volunteers and local staff are involved in establishing an organisation's brand values, as outlined earlier, they should possess a sense of ownership and understand the importance of that brand, both to themselves and the cause which they support. If it is then made easy for them to adopt the brand – providing templates for marketing materials, copies of logos and fonts in multiple electronic formats that can be imported into the most basic word-processing or desktop-publishing programs – they will have little reason to deviate from this.

Above all, it is vital to lead by example. Marketeers must ensure that all centrally organised marketing activities are true to the brand and illustrate well how the brand can be conveyed effectively to different audiences in different circumstances. Once those in the field see what can be achieved through adherence to the brand, they will soon want to follow suit without the need for much coaxing from the centre. Furthermore, the more that local initiatives can reinforce brand values, the more successful national activities will be in distinguishing the cause from the competition.

Naturally, corporate identities may be required to change over time, particularly if a change of charity name is also being considered. Quite often this means retaining the traditional name for legal purposes, but trading under a new name. In this way, the Royal National Lifeboat Institution streamlined its brand from the well-known initials 'RNLI' to, simply, Lifeboats.

A more drastic name change was undertaken by the Spastics Society, when it adopted the new title of Scope in the 1990s. This was as a consequence of the word 'spastic' becoming increasingly used as a term of abuse and as a result service users demanded change. The danger of losing awareness by changing name was far outweighed by the potential damage to the charity's brand values – caring for those with cerebral palsy – if it continued to trade under the old name. Total public awareness did indeed drop from over 90% in 1989/1990 for the Spastics Society to under 50% for the new Scope. By 2001 this had recovered to 71% and while the organisation acknowledges that it is unlikely ever to enjoy the previous high levels, it regards the gains in renewed brand values and support as far outweighing that loss (Hewson 1997; Scope 2001). The stated cost of the complete change was something over £3 million but the real cost in lost donations, lost position and understanding during the intervening years could well have been double that (Hewson 1997). This cost perhaps pales into insignificance when compared to the Royal Mail debacle upon spending £5 million to change its name to Consignia. It had to bear all the costs of changing back less than two years later following massive media criticism and the admission by their new chief executive that the exercise had been a very costly mistake.

Conclusion

We can see how the brand has, in many organisations, become synonymous with the entire offering, encompassing product, values and everything perceived by customers and users. However, in many CSOs and still quite a few major companies, brand values are at odds with those espoused by the organisation and thus public perception is equally inconsistent. Worse still, when employees and supporters do not feel a sense of ownership of shared values it is likely that further confusion and brand fragmentation will arise.

Careful marketing planning can do much to avoid this, but once again integration of those plans, throughout the organisation, is crucial to success. As mentioned in Chapter 1, it may be helpful within CSOs, as Joe Saxton suggests, to substitute the word 'reputation' at every point where one might otherwise talk of 'brand' to volunteers and non-marketing staff. This will help people to understand the value that has been built up in the brand. Rebranding is an exercise to be carried out only after very careful consideration of all the alternatives. It can, however, if there really is no viable alternative, help to meet changed objectives and public perceptions.

CHAPTER FIVE

Shareholder versus stakeholder

There is no formula for success. But there is a formula for failure and that is to try and please everybody.
Nicholas Ray

Pay no attention to what the critics say: no statue has ever been put up to a critic.
Jean Sibelius

This chapter looks at the many audiences that organisations of all types must consider in their marketing activities. It explores how marketing takes place in charities through the conduits of service users and givers and looks at the development and impact of customer loyalty schemes within both commercial organisations and charities. The differences in the make-up and attitudes of key groups defined as stakeholders and shareholders are contrasted and conclusions are drawn about some crucial differences, but also some surprising degrees of overlap. The value to for-profit and not-for-profit organisations of examining more closely how the other achieves success and similarities and differences in achieving that success are explored.

Profits or surpluses?

It is true that one of the first 'laws' of business is that profit must be made. However, this begs the questions for whom and over what time frame? Equally, while most charities would agree that their role is, in some way, to change the status quo, they cannot do that unless they generate sufficient funds to achieve their objectives over time. In order to survive in a fiercely competitive world they are, in reality, compelled to generate surpluses – profits by any other name – so that they can plan ahead, remain solvent and are able to deploy their resources and energy effectively. Thus the question is not so much profits versus change for good but how the profits are deployed and, importantly, who has a real say in the way that those surpluses are generated and dispersed.

In essence, then, both for-profit and not-for-profit organisations seek long-term survival and are dependent upon a range of stakeholders to ensure that survival. As Ansoff (1968) says, for companies 'long-term profitability results from a commitment to understanding the political and social fabric of a community'.

Shareholders

A shareholder is, quite simply, an owner of shares in a company. Therefore, given the nature of not-for-profit organisations, they naturally do not have shareholders in this traditional sense, despite the need to generate surpluses (or profits). However, it can be helpful to see givers to a charity as shareholders. While they hold no shares in the charity (and if there are shares they will be non-tradable and likely to be held in trust by the trustees), since the givers are the very people who fund the charity it is a helpful concept. This idea is explored further in 'The power of investors' on page 80.

There are some interesting observations about company shareholders in relation to ethical and community investment. According to a YouGov survey 45% of UK investors in 2012, when asked about their investing preferences, stated that they would like at least some of their money invested according to green and ethical criteria, and 15% would like to invest all of it in this way. Although these may not at first glance seem to be hugely significant figures, they show a continued rise in the proportion of people with these preferences and this has carried on increasing despite the double-dip recession (Howard 2012). An earlier survey commissioned by Business in the Environment (2001) found that more than half of analysts and two-thirds of investors surveyed believed that a company which emphasises its performance in the area of corporate responsibility is attractive to investors.

In addition, *The Business Case for Corporate Responsibility* (BITC 2003) and the 2010 updated version of the report summarise a number of further surveys of investors to make a strong case for businesses to invest appropriately in corporate responsibility programmes, including work with charities and local community organisations.

Stakeholders

It is generally recognised today that organisations need to consider not only their shareholders or effective owners but also everyone who has an interest, a stake, in the success of that player. Stakeholders can be broadly split into two main types:

1. internal groupings, including employees, management, the board and volunteers (where they exist);

2. external groupings, including customers, users, givers/investors, supporters and prospects.

In addition, of course, there are the opinion influencers such as media commentators, trade institutions and umbrella bodies. Interestingly, other surveys (also summarised in BITC's 2003 and 2010 reports) that have asked customers similar questions to those asked of investors about their preferences have had very similar results. They indicate a public preference in the UK for organisations that are seen to be acting responsibly with society's interests in mind rather than a more limited horizon of maximising shareholder value.

In fact, of course, taking a long-term view of organisational survival, it is not only desirable but probably essential to operate with the public's approval, support and goodwill in order to ensure that all stakeholders, as far as possible, feel some sense of ownership of the organisation. Ownership can take many forms, from the 100% shareholding chief executive and chair of a family business to the individual giver who feels in tune with and a small part of a charity. This sense of participation, however, when widely dispersed, can only help sustain the organisation in the long term.

Case study: NDCS

The case of NDCS (the National Deaf Children's Society) illustrates the importance of ownership and participation well. Formed as a self-help group in 1944 by parents of deaf children, the charity has always worked closely with parents, who still form the majority of its trustees. Increasingly, however, the charity is engaging more directly with deaf young people themselves. The wider communication of shared experiences is enormously beneficial to the organisation and the various participant groups of stakeholders: deaf children, parents, and supporters. Mike Wade, Executive Director of Communications and Fundraising, agrees:

> Every year we work with an Advisory Board made up of deaf young people, who keep us close to deaf youth's experiences. They tell us what is important to them and what they think we should be campaigning on, and we work closely with them to design activities which meet their needs. Keeping close to deaf children also enables us to engage better with supporters. If all members of my team know individual deaf children by name, they are better able to tell their stories, and bring to life for supporters the difference they are making. It's a win-win approach.

NDCS also works internationally to help some of many millions of deaf children in developing countries. Wade continued:

Some of the stories you hear are heartbreaking with deaf children living locked up like animals. We shared their stories with parents of deaf children in the UK and asked them if it was something we should be working on. The fear of course is that it would divert attention away from helping families here, but the message was overwhelming: get out there and do something. So we did.

An interesting example of the interaction between not-for-profit and corporate organisations has been the long standing relationship between NDCS and the Savile Row Shirt company, which has been supporting the charity's overseas work since 2007. Owner Jeffrey Doltis first came into contact with NDCS when his daughter's deafness was identified over 25 years ago. NDCS does a brilliant job for the families of deaf children', says Doltis, 'and I want to support the organisation through my business as much as I possibly can. I also wanted a chance to give something back to the countries I trade with in Asia, where deaf children are dreadfully deprived.'

In the refocus of its objects to provide mobility support for blind people, Guide Dogs (formerly Guide Dogs for the Blind) may have achieved a similar impact to that NDCS has for givers and potential supporters. Formerly the charity was seen simply as a provider of guide dogs for blind people. Unfortunately only some 4,000 people could be helped in this way at any one time, leading to an enormous gulf between public perceptions and the reality of service provision. Media stories during the early 2000s about the charity's substantial reserves exacerbated the situation. The refocus and dramatic broadening of the organisation's work coincided with a much more proactive approach to fundraising to address both the deficits which the charity had been running, partly in an attempt to address criticisms of its reserves as well to fund the expanded nature and scope of the work. This revised picture enabled the organisation to work more closely with groups of stakeholders, especially supporters, and create a platform for development in the twenty-first century.

Case study: RNLI

The RNLI has also faced the issue of being perceived to have large reserves and the need to reconcile highly effective fundraising with changing public perceptions. Ian Ventham, the former head of fundraising, helped to persuade the charity of the opportunity it had to broaden its work which would, coincidentally, improve the fundraising proposition. Thus, while the core mission remained to provide a lifeboat service to save lives at sea, the RNLI took on the additional tasks of life guarding, rescue services on inland waters and help with flood relief, both in the British Isles and overseas.

These new tasks have not been without difficulties and challenges. A conservative supporter base had to be persuaded that the new activities did not detract from the traditional and much-respected work of the lifeboat crews. Lifeguarding brought with it the challenge of working with local authorities and in partnership with two established charities in the lifeguarding field, Royal Lifesaving Society and Surf Life Saving Association. Sending a rapid response team to Mozambique in 2001 brought the organisation into contact with DFID (the Department for International Development) for the first time. Working on inland waters and in flood relief situations in UK and Ireland challenged traditional ways of working and highlighted different training needs for crews. Crucially some of these new activities required the RNLI to amend its governing document, its Royal Charter.

Perhaps the biggest challenge, though, was to plan and execute complex internal and external marketing and communication strategies to explain, justify and sell the expanding role of the charity. The stakeholders ranged from trustees to crew members, and from the Charity Commission to many district councils. There are also a small number of independent lifeboat associations, and so the process is far from over.

In each of these cases the organisations have endeavoured to make their cause come alive for new and existing stakeholder groups, which in turn provides greater support and improved services to the beneficiary groups. These are examples of the virtuous circle of communication where change that is well executed and communicated has a further impact on communications, which in turn assists the change process.

The role of the consumer

One of the things marketeers need to do in order to understand the various agendas and interests held by differing groups of stakeholders is to become a part of that group. Strategies for developing and improving approval levels can be informed by and developed using the understanding gleaned from doing so. Commercial organisations frequently invest in 'professional shoppers', 'mystery customers' and unannounced visits/inspections to try to gauge and mirror customer reactions to the buying experience. Fundraisers can gain very valuable giver experiences by becoming one. Using a false name if necessary, it is very instructive to be on the receiving end of the sometimes apparently endless communications from your own charity.

Similarly, it is worth trying to buy something from one of your own shops or outlets or participate, as a punter, in an organised fundraising or sponsorship activity. This approach can be taken further. By trying to experience the customer care of other charities that are operating within the same sector, you can gain valuable feedback and make comparisons in order to improve your own charity's organisational responses, communications and received perceptions.

An important difference between many for-profit and not-for-profit organisations is that the end-user or consumer is quite different from the actual purchaser or customer. For example, Leonard Cheshire's customers are generally local authorities and health trusts while the service users are a wide range of disabled people. Clearly, while social work staff must work closely with their clients, the authorities' priorities may be quite different from those of the disabled people themselves. The charity can become stuck in the middle in trying to deliver services that the service users want; for example, appropriate support where and when people with disabilities want it, while the cash-strapped purchasers are seeking to minimise costs and the resources to be expended on the support. Mutually incompatible priorities are hard to reconcile but marketeers must put themselves in the shoes of both groups if they are to develop a clear understanding in order to improve their own performance.

Customers as advocates

It is well recognised that genuine testimonials from satisfied customers have always been a valuable part of establishing credibility in the minds of prospective customers or clients. Anecdotal evidence suggests that while a satisfied customer may, unprompted, recommend a product or service to perhaps six or eight acquaintances, dissatisfied customers tell 20 or more – underlining the need to build upon and actively use the experiences of clients who are content with the experience they have received. Indeed, as mentioned in Chapter 10, with the increased access to EWOM (electronic word of mouth) via social networking sites the dissatisfied customer may now tell 2000 people of the bad experience (Roberts and Barker 2010).

With regard to positive feedback, fundraisers have the opportunity to go a step further. Provided that a CSO is meeting the needs of its service users, their experiences can be used very effectively to underpin a fundraising approach. Whether it is photographs of rescued animals or the quotations from beneficiaries who have positive messages, the impact can be similarly powerful. Equally there is no need to descend into the 'triumph over tragedy' outdated models of charity fundraising. Continuing advertisements showing starving babies may elicit some immediate guilt-inspired donations but will do little to engender a long-term relationship. Honest, positive experiences can be used with much greater effect, though it is recognised that much more work in developing the case for support and then recording appropriate experience will be needed.

Case study: Arthritis Care

Arthritis Care spent a significant amount of time and energy in developing internal guidelines for the use of user experiences within the direct marketing programme. It is easy but very short-sighted to fall into the trap of using 'heroes in adversity' stories which, although initially attention-grabbing, demean the users themselves and often, over time, turn supporters and potential givers away from the very cause that is seeking help.

Instead of going down this route, in 2000 the charity developed a four-point checklist that any message coming from fundraising needed to be positive, honest, powerful and urgent. Powerful, urgent messages were needed to change perceptions of the 'non-life-threatening', 'just a symptom of old age' nature of arthritis. Positive did not mean that the full impact of severe arthritis in childhood could not be portrayed but that the outcomes would be a key part of the message to avoid turning people with arthritis into 'victims'. Honesty was also crucial to avoid promising a cure but showing how information, empowerment and the right support can make all the difference to someone who has arthritis – at any age.

The impact over time was significant; more users accepted the validity of the advertising, communications and fundraising activities and were willing to be portrayed themselves. In turn this led to a greater understanding by supporters and a significant uplift in long-term support.

Cancer charities have been adopting a similar approach to Arthritis Care with much greater emphasis on the long-term impacts of interventions on those overcoming cancer to persuade givers to give on a long-term basis. The turnaround is neatly summed up in the quote used in press and direct-response television (DRTV) advertising that having cancer is about life, not death. It was the threat of death which until recently was the big scare factor that mobilised millions of people to give hundreds of millions of pounds towards cancer research and care. The lessons which are relevant to for-profit organisations lie in the life-affirming nature of such projects and the value that can be added to commercial brands through working with appropriate CSOs. The positive attitudes and experiences espoused by organisations are reflected in enhanced values and reputations.

The power of investors

Within commercial organisations investors are usually shareholders who expect a reasonable return on investment through stock dividends and growth in share values. As we have seen, however, those same investors can value other attributes highly, such as an organisation's contribution to its local community.

Shareholders can exert enormous power upon a board of directors, particularly in cases where acquisitions and mergers come into play. Large shareholders, usually institutional (and often pension funds), are courted and kept well informed as to the intentions and plans of the organisation. This preoccupation with share value is not always a healthy one when, as in the case of Worldcom, Enron and Xerox, it leads to fraudulent declarations of profits in order to maintain inflated share values.

In charities, givers are sometimes seen to be more like a company's shareholders rather than customers of a particular CSO. They provide much of the funding for the work of the organisation and fundraising departments are charged with maintaining good relations, keeping them well informed and happy with the work of the charity. However, there is a potential dissonance. Supporters receive no dividends, yet without their continued incoming investment the charity will (usually) run out of funds all too soon. The cultivation, therefore, of long-term supporters as investors as opposed to regarding them simply as customers can be very helpful to the survival and long-term health of a CSO. Lessons from the good practices of commercial organisations need to be learned and adopted in suitable formats to fit the differing attitudes, perceptions and needs of shareholders over supporters. Chapter 9 goes into more detail about the needs and motivations of individual givers and how best to cultivate long-term relationships.

Increasingly, the communications functions within companies are including responsibility for investor relations, often under the guise of corporate affairs. Meetings and briefings for larger institutional investors are being enhanced by improved shareholder communications, not relying simply on the annual report and accounts, the AGM and dividends, interim or final. Great effort is made to ensure that the press are briefed ahead of profit forecasts or warnings. Takeovers, mergers and acquisitions present particular challenges for companies to inform investors effectively, building confidence, understanding and feelings of shared ownership. With the current climate of reduced funding it is likely that many more CSOs will contemplate mergers and acquisitions with the consequent need to adopt and adapt the best practices used by commercial investor communicators. Indeed those best practices are valuable whenever organisations attempt to communicate news of significant changes.

Communicating with investors

Good fundraisers already spend much time talking to givers in an effort to understand how they want to hear about the charity's progress, but almost inevitably those charged with direct marketing cannot resist adding an additional 'ask' to giver communication, however soft, however polite. While in the past this may have raised the number of unprompted donations, there is a real risk of alienating long-term supporters permanently. 'They only ever write to me for money' is an all too familiar response to communications, especially welcome packs – beloved of direct marketing agencies for creating instant uplifts for minimal investment.

The ubiquitous charity questionnaire, apparently asking for a supporter's (or a potential supporter's) views but in reality a giving recruitment or enhancement device, is one piece of direct mail that is still in widespread use. It is, however, perhaps nearing the end of its effective life due to overuse and misuse. A Macmillan Cancer 2002 door-drop included a letter from the chief executive asking for help so that the organisation understands, '...a little bit about you and your experiences on cancer care...' it went on to ask for a modest gift of £2 per month. A banker's order was attached to the questionnaire. The inevitable free pen was enclosed. The ask was made despite the recipient being a long-term, occasional supporter of the charity. It was acknowledged of course that this is a cold recruitment pack seeking first-time support, but how much more effective it might have been to make a request for support *after* receipt of the returned questionnaire; the monetary request could then have been accompanied by feedback on the results of the survey and an explanation of how these results will be used within the organisation. If supporters' views are genuinely sought, valued and used to determine policy, making an immediate request for money to accompany answers must significantly reduce response rates, even if the initial return on investment is much higher.

Despite the shortcomings of this particular communication – which in similar forms is used by dozens of major charities in their fundraising programmes – it is fair to comment that Macmillan Cancer has an enviable reputation for its efforts to engage givers and enlist active support. Judy Beard, previously director of fundraising at the charity, commented, 'we feel the pack has served its purpose and are testing alternative propositions with a view to replacing it as soon as we can find a viable replacement' (personal communication 2002).

By contrast, a Friends of the Earth door-drop in 2002, signed by its chief executive Charles Secret, cut straight to the point stating that it was the cheapest, most effective way of talking to people about urgent issues needing regular donations to help make a difference. The pen was still there as an 'uplift device' but it felt a much more honest, open approach. In the same vein at that time, a door-drop from Cancer

Research UK included a pen to help fill in the response form but was completely transparent, having asked on the outer envelope, 'how much does it cost to litter your doorstep?' The letter then went on to admit that the cost to send the unaddressed letter was 13p and continued justifying that investment with refreshing candour. A more recent example is a Christmas fundraising letter from St Mungo's in 2012 that contained a more thoughtful uplift device, enclosing some gift tags which its chief executive, Charles Fraser, stated 'only cost a few pence to produce, and are a small token of appreciation for your support', the idea being that they would be used on presents for friends and family, who would think of a homeless person 'who's being given a warm welcome – thanks to your generosity'.

Probably one of the worst examples around, however, was from the World Villages for Children, an American organisation that was fundraising very successfully in the UK in 2002 by sending addressed cold packs with 12p actually stuck on the letter. The letter went on to ask for the recipient to add £10 and send back £10.12p to feed a child for a week. The marketing director, when taxed about the honesty and ethical nature of this type of approach, could only retreat behind a barrage of 'but it works' rhetoric. In 2005 the charity upped the ante by sending out umbrellas, unsolicited, to potential givers and this was investigated by both the Advertising Standards Authority and the Charity Commission (ASA 2008). In 2009 the Fundraising Standards Board also investigated complaints. Perhaps most revealing is a report on the Charity Commission website showing income of £6.6 million and fundraising costs of £2.6 million – a 40% cost ratio, while the organisation apparently only employs three people (Charity Commission 2010, 2011).

In this context perhaps a much more effective piece of genuine supporter/investor communication would be a questionnaire that is aimed at understanding how the supporter actually wants to hear from the charity. As discussed in Chapter 1, Botton Village (part of the Camphill Trust), a project for people with learning difficulties, did this with enormous success. Having asked supporters whether they wanted to hear, once, twice, four times, twelve times per year (or whenever), the fundraisers then made sure that communications, fundraising or otherwise, fitted the requested pattern (Stroud 1995).

The Internet is providing innovative cost-effective ways of enhancing investor communications. Oxfam has spent significant time and effort establishing which supporters prefer to receive email information – and how often. Fundraising asks made as a part of an overall communications plan should produce better results over time even if initial returns on investment are lower. Charities must be particularly mindful of the need to satisfy supporters. It is only through long-term support from givers who are happy with what the organisation is achieving and who feel part of or some ownership of its cause that the charities themselves will succeed with legacy-development programmes. It is these programmes that are now forming a crucial part of an increasing number of fundraising strategies.

Creating ownership of a cause or brand

In developing a sense of ownership of a cause or brand and its inherent values it is useful, as already discussed, to bring a cross-section of stakeholders together, inviting representatives from each group on the strength of their ability to champion the emerging values among their peers and colleagues. Once brought together in this way, stakeholders can be asked to share their views on the organisation, allowing participants to express their emotional response to an organisation in a tangible, understandable way. For charities to put givers, service users, volunteers and staff in the same room might feel rather threatening. Properly facilitated, however, the results could prove invaluable and the resulting advocates are likely to energise many of their colleagues and friends.

Focus groups must be carefully structured and balanced. Thought must be given to the make-up and individual participants. If an experienced professional agency is not used then the facilitator must brief the group really carefully, ensuring agreement to the form and format. Enough time to allow participants to interact and engage is crucial if the group is to produce useful results. Meaningful feedback, of the results and their impact, for the individuals who were involved is an important but often-overlooked vehicle to ensure continued support and to help develop brand champions.

While paper and online surveys can prove a useful alternative, they cannot fully reproduce the emotional responses and feedback that can be elicited through focus groups, or even informal feedback sessions. Once again, all respondents must feel that their replies will genuinely influence the process. Whatever methods are used to involve stakeholders, it is unlikely that the values which emerge will be totally alien or unexpected to anybody. As has been discussed, charitable causes, very like brands, are a distillation of the attitudes, perceptions and values that come from within the organisation, and anyone who works for or supports a particular cause is likely to have great empathy with some if not all of those attitudes and values. Values that seem to be imposed from outside will not only seem alien to stakeholders but those values are likely to be at odds with those perceived by the observers.

Work to develop brand champions needs to be based firmly on the results of empirical research such as the focus groups suggested rather than on the assumptions of those charged with fundraising or even on the input of trustees alone. At best an incomplete picture will result and at worst the risk of alienation and claims of outdated views or unworldly expectations are likely to result. Any communication plan ought to devote significant resources to the development and subsequent use of such brand champions. This must then also include champions among the most senior of stakeholders, directors and trustees.

The board

Chapter 3 draws attention to the need not only for thorough planning but also for the knowledge of those plans and their implementation to be fully communicated within the organisation. Too many marketing strategies and plans, while excellent on paper, fail to get beyond first or second base because stakeholders (including, crucially, powerful stakeholders such as board members) lose confidence or allow other considerations to intrude during the inevitable refinement periods that follow a new programme or activity plan.

Naturally these 'second thoughts' are not confined to marketing programmes but, being a very visible manifestation of an organisation's intentions, the implementation of marketing plans is likely to come under the most scrutiny and criticism. Boards of commercial organisations are not driven purely by stated and apparently agreed corporate objectives. The debacle of British Airways tailplanes is a good case in point. Agreement at a senior level to commission modern artists to repaint the tail fins of the BA fleet, at significant cost, evaporated in the face of strident public criticism by the then Prime Minister, Margaret Thatcher. An even more costly reversion to union flag colours followed. A similar debacle occurred in 2004 when Coca-Cola launched a 'new' type of bottled water under the brand name Dasani. When it was shown to contain nothing but tap water the product was hastily withdrawn. CSOs are, however, even more likely to reject a marketing initiative prematurely if marketing continues to be seen as an interloper from the commercial realm and not really relevant to the world of charity.

Champions within the trustee body must be wholly behind new programmes of, say, fundraising investment. Typically, these are plans that will see a concerted increase in investment over four or five years, usually in an effort to improve the funding mix by reducing reliance on a single revenue source and increasing the availability of unrestricted funds to allow the organisation to increase its investment in the provision of core services. Often such programmes produce negative cash flow over two or three years. It is then easy for boards which are not fully behind such programmes, or for influential individuals on those boards who do not fully understand their ramifications, to begin criticising, interfering and ultimately changing direction away from the agreed strategy. This will almost inevitably be at great cost to the organisation and allows a knee-jerk reaction in the face of criticism and ignorance to divert the charity from its purpose.

Senior managers have a responsibility to ensure unanimity of attitude towards such programmes. They must show resolution in the face of criticism. Preparation for and contingency plans to counter antipathy may be a very necessary part of the implementation process. When the NSPCC launched the Full Stop campaign it did so to the accompaniment of considerable media comment and voluntary sector scepticism. However, internally everyone from the trustees and senior managers down to individual staff and volunteers working in all sections, service delivery, administration, finance and fundraising had bought into 'the big idea'. That was the mission to put an end to child cruelty. So far, while external pundits carp about timescales and cost ratios, the organisation is able to remain true to its purpose, which is evidence of clear and effective internal communications (personal communication 2012). Giles Pegram, the director responsible for setting and ultimately achieving the £250 million target, can take much of the credit for this. The model is worthy of replication.

Conclusion

It can be seen from the preceding examples and descriptions that both commercial and not-for-profit organisations need stakeholder approval to operate most effectively. Careful consideration of who makes up this complex group is most important in considering the appropriate communications strategy to adopt.

Without this approval, companies and charities will always struggle to communicate their values and ethos properly. One very effective way to improve that approval – the buy-in factor – is to promote closer working partnerships between for-profit and not-for-profit organisations which share values in their community involvement, corporate affairs and marketing activities. This is explored further in the next chapter.

CHAPTER SIX

Volunteers – the unique benefit proposition

People who never get carried away should be.
Malcolm Forbes

They laughed at Joan of Arc but she went right ahead . . .
Gracie Allan

Volunteers are the very lifeblood of charities, and are one of the defining differences between for-profit and not-for-profit organisations. This chapter explores the unique input and involvement of volunteers and examines how they can play a vital part in any successful marketing approach. It shows how volunteers can become champions of brand values, which in turn reinforces the importance of internal leadership and commitment. Also examined is the fact that, while in commercial organisations few employees would consider themselves as volunteers, many will volunteer as part of their company's community affairs programmes to work with charities, which in turn can bring enormous benefits to both organisations.

Considering supporters and volunteers

One of the reasons why people support charities is for religious motivation. All the major religions teach the support and care of our neighbours. Thus many charities have their roots in religious motivation, even if today they are secular in the way in which they operate.

CSOs with such origins do, of course, continue to derive support on a wide scale from their natural constituencies. Islamic Relief (2012), for example, states that it allocates its resources 'regardless of race, political affiliation, gender or belief'. The propensity to support through monetary gifts remains high among those with active religious beliefs (Stothart 2012).

However, research from the Department for Communities and Local Government (2011), NCVO (2007) and the Cabinet Office (Low et al. 2007) shows that there is little difference in levels of volunteering between religious and non-religious people. The word charity itself, derived from the Greek *caritas*, refers to a love of humanity, which is, of course, not limited to religious people, but covers anyone who would consider themselves to be a humanist, whether formally or informally.

Case study: Brooke Hospital for Animals

The Brooke Hospital for Animals was founded in 1934 by Dorothy Brooke in response to the enormous suffering she saw first-hand in Cairo (Searight 1993). She saw that thousands of ex-cavalry horses, sold off by the British Army at the end of the First World War, were still being literally worked to death 16 years later. She wrote a letter to the *Morning Post*, which brought in the equivalent of £20,000 to enable 'something to be done'. An attempt to provide care and support for these animals through an animal hospital and rest facility called The Cairo War Horse Memorial Hospital rapidly expanded into a free veterinary service for working equines when the extent of the problems of poor animal care, ignorance and poverty was appreciated. The organisation in 2012 operates as the Brooke and has more than 140 vets in 10 countries. Around one million treatments are administered each year and the charity has ambitious plans through outreach and education projects (the Brooke 2012).

Typically supporters have very quietly given quite large amounts over extended periods of time, once they have visited one of the clinics. The motivation is prompted by a love of animals, in particular horses, donkeys and mules, but there is evidence that a high percentage of active supporters, who also participate in fundraising events and visits, are also active churchgoers. Thus the Brooke Hospital for Animals has, perhaps unknowingly, drawn enormous long-term support by finding synergy between the organisation's beliefs and values, and those of its supporters.

Volunteers – stakeholders or shareholders?

Can volunteers be thought of as stakeholders and/or shareholders or do they need a different approach for support?

Bruce (2011) usefully defines stakeholders as those who have legitimacy and power over the running of a charity – thus strengthening the analogy between stakeholders and shareholders (as outlined in Chapter 5). However, he goes on to say that therefore beneficiaries (and by extension volunteers) are not stakeholders in any legal or realistic sense. He adds, however, that *representatives* of beneficiaries, if recognised by the charity, are indeed stakeholders.

This is a limited view. In practical terms it would be much more helpful to consider all the involved groups – trustees, staff, beneficiaries, supporters, givers and volunteers – as stakeholders with an interest and investment, however intangible, in the organisation.

Certainly for communications planning, volunteers need to be considered and thought of as having a real interest in what the organisation plans to do and how it executes its intentions.

Founders as volunteers

Most businesses are started by an individual or small group of people who have a particular idea that might make money or interest in an activity that they are keen to attempt professionally. Sometimes it is even a vision about how things might be. When Steve Jobs and Steve Wozniak built the first Apple computers in their garage in 1976, they did not just have an idea which they thought might make money. They foresaw the advantages of every home having a computer and this vision drove them on to seek venture capital from friends and build a business now worth billions of dollars worldwide. Jobs' death in 2011 prompted many obituarists to reinforce the notion the he had indeed continued to be a visionary after leaving and then rejoining Apple.

In a not dissimilar way those who are driven to found charities do so usually from a deep conviction that a need must be met or the world changed in some way for the better. They 'volunteer' their services to this end.

Case study: Leonard Cheshire

Founding a charity was probably the last thing on Leonard Cheshire's mind in 1948. He was living at the time in a large, run-down country house trying to stave off bankruptcy after a failed venture. The matron of his local cottage hospital approached him and asked if he would consider giving a home to a man called Arthur Dykes who was dying of liver cancer. Dykes had worked for a short time as a pigman with Cheshire in the failed self-sufficiency project. The matron told Cheshire that the doctors had done all they could for Dykes and that she needed his hospital bed for others. To coin a familiar modern phrase, he was bed blocking.

Cheshire was appalled that there was no provision for someone like Dykes in the National Health Service. He contacted a string of charities and organisations providing support for ex-servicemen on Dykes' behalf but none would take him. So Cheshire reluctantly agreed to look after Dykes himself – at the run-down country house.

During the few weeks that Cheshire, with no experience or training, nursed Dykes, word of his altruism spread and following Dykes' death the house, Le Court in rural Hampshire, was filled with a variety of terminally ill people and tuberculosis patients. Importantly, there were also younger disabled people who, though not ill, had no provision available and were often stuck in totally unsuitable cottage hospitals or nursing homes for the elderly. Cheshire sought help from family and friends and within months the eponymous charity was formed with a separate management committee drawn from a wide range of contacts. More homes followed and the decision to work principally with disabled people rather than the terminally ill developed directly out of Cheshire's own growing interest in making a difference to the lives of younger people for whom no specialist provision then existed.

As the charity's first volunteer, Cheshire was admirably placed to win support and help from others. His charisma was extraordinary and he in turn could inspire people to volunteer their help when they had no intention, initially, of becoming involved. As Cheshire's biographer Richard Morris (2000) puts it, Air Vice Marshal Sir Christopher Foxley-Norris (former chair of The Leonard Cheshire Foundation) revealed that he had absolutely no intention of becoming a trustee yet found himself agreeing after a conversation terminated by Cheshire with the words, '...good, well I'm glad that's settled then'.

Another example of the power of Cheshire's presence and personal impact occurred some years later when he was attempting to help Indian colleagues to set up a Cheshire Home near Delhi. A suitable piece of land had been identified but its acquisition was directly against the newly independent government's policy. Cheshire secured an interview with the Prime Minister, Pandit Nehru, but spent the entire time seemingly tongue-tied. As David Lean the film-maker, who happened to be with him in India, explains, Leonard hardly said a word all afternoon. But when the time to leave came, Nehru asked how Cheshire would get back to his hotel. He replied that he'd probably get the bus and then walk. Nehru then did an unheard of thing and summoned his own car and driver to take them back. He waved goodbye and then turned to his aides saying, 'There goes the greatest man I've met since Gandhi. Give him what he wants!' (Morris 2000).

Founders are often difficult people to work with. They have a clear vision and mission and are often completely single-minded, acting as though they are totally certain of achieving their objectives. They usually inspire employees who join them early in a venture but sometimes frustrate their staff as the organisation grows.

Moving on from the founder's vision

Organisations and the people working within them tend, generally, to mimic or at least repeat the behaviour of their leaders. After all, that is the model of success, so why push water uphill? Yet in not-for-profit and for-profit organisations alike, the transition from leadership by the founder to a delegated board with chairs and chief executives can be traumatic and is rarely smooth. In Cheshire's case, he made the transition unusually easy. His drive to continue exploring new areas and to assist projects around the world meant that he both needed and was able to allow others to manage.

Yet twenty years after his death the charity still derives inspiration from his vision. In 1975, with characteristic foresight, he made a film called *Thoughts for the Future*. This remarkable recording urges trustees, staff and volunteers to go on meeting unmet need and never to shirk a decision that needs to be made by saying 'Leonard wouldn't have approved'. That was 17 years before he died. Today the charity works as Leonard Cheshire Disability, having dropped the Foundation tag to underline the service-provision aspects of its work and prevent confusion with grantmaking trusts. In adding the word 'disability' it has attempted to underline the most important group of all, its beneficiaries.

The organisation itself reports that in 2011/12 more than 17,500 people entered school or work, campaigned or received rehabilitation services through its international projects in 54 countries around the world. It has more than 3,000 active volunteers who gave nearly half a million hours of their time in 2011/12, offering help ranging from sitting on local committees to driving, visiting, supporting individuals and, of course, fundraising (LCD 2012).

Cheshire's wife, Sue Ryder, was the founder of her own charity which offers palliative care and was, many feel, one of the forerunners of the modern hospice movement. Sadly the transition from her own leadership to that of the board and management was very acrimonious, leading to her resignation and the formation of yet another charity to pursue her humanitarian objectives called the Bouverie Foundation (*The Telegraph* 2000). Today the Sue Ryder Foundation, operating as Sue Ryder, still has the support of thousands of loyal volunteers inspired by Ryder but who continue to work within the organisation still bearing her name. The 400 charity shops have been rebranded to present a consistent message with greater clarity, to both supporters and the public. Awareness campaigns have sought to challenge public perceptions about the work of the organisation and the people who use its services in order to underpin that move towards better understanding and support.

Many organisations experience significant pain in moving from control by the founder to, usually, a more devolved style of management board with professionals exercising their functional skill more strategically. Kay-Williams (2000) has written a fascinating thesis on the various stages of voluntary organisations' fundraising and highlights the important evolutionary steps that effective organisations must negotiate successfully, including the step changes from the first employee to that of a full staff team doing most of what the volunteer board formally did.

Employees as volunteers

While many people in commercial organisations volunteer to work additional hours or attend extra events without pay, they are nevertheless paid members of staff. The motivation for such personal participation might more usually be identified as status enhancement, skill development, team assistance and personal reward by helping the organisation to perform more effectively. Philanthropy is rarely the motivating force.

However, the opportunities to enjoy all of those factors and many more altruistic ones exist when the volunteering within the workplace is part of a project to work with CSOs. Many good examples exist, from The Conservation Volunteers (TCV) which, among its various activities, puts together teams of volunteers from corporate participants to work on conservation projects, to Business in the Community which is dedicated to encouraging companies to seek out community partners and assist them via employee volunteering schemes. When these are linked with marketing initiatives a much greater synergy can be achieved through shared branding and fundraising activities, utilising both staff volunteering input and revenue generation via trading and cause-related marketing. Once again a more integrated approach – from both types of organisation – can result in large increases in added value.

The changing face of the volunteer

A survey conducted by *The Guardian* shows that working for a charity is a top choice among men and women. The UK-wide survey conducted among workers (aged 25 to 70) revealed that a surprising 22% of those surveyed would like to work for a charity 'if they could shed the shackles of their everyday job' (O'Hara 2002). This reveals a fascinating opportunity for charities to provide far more volunteering and secondment opportunities to corporate partners, supporting the government's efforts to promote volunteering and greater participation in and with the voluntary sector. There must surely be creative opportunities for charities to seize, providing innovative volunteering to fit both sets of objectives.

Perhaps what is needed now is not just opportunities for an individual or team to enhance their expertise and people skills but also for human resource departments working on staff development programmes to take account of their employees' desires and ambitions. They need to seek creative long-term relationships with CSOs where they offer both people and marketing activities so as to both raise funds and create additional operational capacity to deliver services. This works whether it is to improve the environment through education campaigns or to enhance the lives of those experiencing discrimination, disaffection and dislocation. Shared values and an increase in public awareness and understanding of such projects could only benefit the commercial and not-for-profit organisations' objectives mutually.

The beneficiaries

The previous chapter explored the roles of various stakeholders but it is worth considering the *volunteer* role that beneficiaries, in particular, can play for charities and how that differs from the non-monetary contribution customers can make to commercial organisations as part of focus groups or as product champions in return for some purchasing loyalty.

The beneficiaries of the services provided by CSOs are rarely customers as such, and their relationship with the service provider is therefore likely to be profoundly different even where the user is not the purchaser (as with the National Health Service). However, earlier models of grateful, needy clients gaining benefit from a charity's intervention are, not before time, giving way to client consultation, empowerment programmes and active participation in governance by service users. Arthritis Care's board of trustees moved from having 48 members, few with personal experience of arthritis, to one in 2000 that had 17 members, the majority of whom, including the chair, having the condition. Cancer and other disability care charities might consider how they could achieve the same levels of user participation. Trustees are not generally remunerated, so motivation to make a difference, as a volunteer, has to be very high indeed.

The members

Many CSOs, such as Arthritis Care and Action on Hearing Loss (formerly RNID), are membership organisations. In sporting organisations members are usually the principal stakeholders, being both the beneficiaries and the funders. Volunteer involvement and marketing challenges, however, remain much the same as for other CSOs.

Case study: England Hockey

England Hockey (formerly The English Hockey Association) depends upon the affiliation fees from the clubs around the country. Some 106,000 adults continue to play hockey in England (England Hockey 2012). The overwhelming majority of people playing are of course amateur; each affiliated club is run by and for amateurs and these volunteers resent any investment not seen as directly benefiting the game and participating players. Yet the EHA became insolvent in 2002 because it could not handle the large amounts of funds flowing into the game through grant assistance from Sport UK. Sadly, Andrew Hope, an old friend of the author, died in the summer of 2011, but while he was the interim chief executive he commented: 'The challenge is to create an infrastructure that can then deliver on facilities, pitches, coaching and player development, whilst being seen by the clubs as relevant and of benefit to them.' He went on: 'Hockey must be marketed as an exciting, family sport. The integration of the men's, women's and mixed sections means we can promote this exciting but non-contact sport to all ages' (personal communication 2002).

Certainly the sport has moved on since mixed hockey was played by many at university on rough, pitted grass pitches, but success in the 1980s when the England team were world champions was not translated into club membership, improved facilities or increased corporate support. The infrastructure is being put into place, but can the former success at an international level be repeated?

Moreover, without international success how can major corporate support be obtained? Hope continued: 'It's true that money often follows such international success but there are alternatives. Success at a family participation level and the backing of high-profile champions or ambassadors may mean we can interest major brands aimed directly at the family to join with us in growing the sport.'

Commercial partners

There remains a huge stigma attached to volunteers as amateurs compared to professionals who are paid and often have impressive qualifications to back their claims of competence and expertise. Conversely, within trustee bodies there is often a dismissive attitude bordering upon contempt for staff and management as 'the hired help' who, by definition, cannot be as committed as volunteers who give their time for free. Staff on the other hand may not think of their trustees as volunteers at all. Sometimes it may be seen almost as a class issue, with the board packed by well-educated upper-middle-class people. This is a debate not usually experienced by the corporate sector; nevertheless, it is highly relevant when it comes to the use of voluntary assistance by the staff of a commercial partner to a charity. These are, it should be remembered, staff who are often highly qualified and experienced in their professional roles. They are people who are likely to become rapidly demotivated and uninterested unless they feel valued, have a sense that they are making a real contribution and, particularly important, are listened to if they make comments and suggestions.

From a marketing perspective the opportunity to use such assistance, whether corporate or individual, or from the local community, is a wonderful one when it can be integrated properly into the communications plan. Volunteer experiences along with those of service users provide invaluable public relations, and those same people go on to be long-term champions of the cause, expounding their enthusiasm to anyone who will listen. At this level there is real benefit in corporate fundraisers investing significant time and resources into developing friends and supporters within target companies and those already beginning to work with a charity.

Trustees

Trustee boards, as noted, differ in one essential aspect from the boards of directors of for-profit organisations: the members are unpaid (though expenses are usually reimbursed). Trustees, like their motivations, come in all shapes and sizes. Many have begun by volunteering with the organisation because they have an affinity with the cause and (more usually) because a friend, colleague or relative asked them to help.

Just as with company directors, trustees have a prime governance and policy role and are legally responsible for the probity of the organisation.

Case studies: trustees

SL, a retired officer, became involved at a local level with a national charity through his knowledge and subsequent work in estate agency. Several years of serving successfully on a local committee led to his being approached by an existing trustee who had succession planning on his mind. SL accepted a position on the public affairs committee and subsequently became its chair and was invited to join the board of trustees. While charities are increasingly consulting memberships (where they exist) and establishing electoral systems to improve representation within governing structures, the experiences of SL remain typical of many. Both national charities and the majority of small local CSOs often struggle to secure a sufficient quality and quantity of trustees able to operate effectively within the increasingly complex environment of the twenty-first century.

JT, a senior manager at BT, was on the receiving end of a periodic reorganisation and took early retirement in his fifties. Within six months he had felt the need for the stimulation of work but he had not actively pursued any volunteer links or opportunities.

However, a former colleague who was with the Prince's Trust recognised that JT's strategic and financial management skills were just waiting to be harnessed. An invitation to a networking event followed and the director of a small student volunteering charity, Student Volunteering UK, made an approach through the mutual friend. At that time the charity was known as SCADU and had a turnover of just £100,000. The volunteer unit at the Home Office was the largest single funder and was concerned about its financial planning. The unit needed someone with good financial planning skills on the trustee board. JT was interested in the concept, liked the idea of working with younger people and could, critically, understand how his existing skills and talents might be used to help the organisation.

Six years later the charity had repositioned itself, changed its name, was turning over £500,000 and had a growing student support network. While it would be unfair to ascribe all this to the contribution of one trustee, the fact is that the growth and success went hand in glove with a dynamic new director, a revitalised board and clear financial planning. Significantly, JT persuaded the organisation to introduce time limits for length of trustee service. He himself was then faced with succession planning and at the same time a new director had been appointed and retirement beckoned for him, although, as he said, 'retiring as a trustee doesn't mean I lose interest in the organisation though whether I'll pursue other volunteering roles in this or another organisation remains to be seen.'

In fact, he went on to become the trustee treasurer of Mind, following an open advertisement.

Increasingly, CSOs are finding it helpful to set time limits on the length of service and many have open elections to ensure that anyone interested in serving has an opportunity to put themselves forward, rather than wait to be asked. One young woman joined the youth section of a national charity that deals with the condition which she had. As an active, committed volunteer she quickly became known to other members and was elected chair of the youth section. With that role came a place on the main trustee board and over time her skills, passion and commitment resulted in her being elected chair of the main charity. She, as an elected chair, is still, however, very much the exception.

Trustees should be the most committed supporters that a charity has. In the USA trustees are expected to contribute regularly to the cause, not just their time, but financially at whatever level they are able to give. In the UK this is much rarer and service is often seen as an alternative to significant financial support. Yet how many companies would expect to have non-shareholding directors? As referred to in the previous chapter, trustees have a responsibility to understand plans they ask managers to implement and to stand by those plans, reviewing necessary refinements but sticking with strategy once it has been agreed by the organisation.

Marketeers in CSOs need to work very closely with their chief executives to gain acceptance and understanding by the entire trustee body of the need to engage with the marketing process and realise the true value locked into the organisation's reputation. In turn trustees have to embrace the changes that this involves and understand that their roles change along with the organisation. This in turn can mean very significant shifts in the types of people becoming trustees and the ways in which they interact.

Conclusion

As outlined in Chapter 4, customers and investors show preferences for commercial brands supporting community investment, in line with Ansoff's arguments. This surely is an indicator that many for-profit companies could improve reputations and public perceptions by participating more fully as volunteers in community concerns. Moreover, through active, well-resourced marketing programmes they could collaborate more productively with appropriate CSOs.

Volunteers can be seen to be the UBP (unique benefit proposition) for charities, replacing the USP (unique selling proposition) of the commercial world. One has only to think of the purple-clad volunteers adding a special touch to the 2012 Olympic Games in London to see what a huge difference well-trained and well-deployed volunteers can make. Skilled corporate practitioners would be wise to make use of both the UBP and the USP in order to enhance their marketing programmes and develop their brands.

CHAPTER SEVEN

Marketing communications – media or message?

> *The medium is the message.*
> Marshall McLuhan

> *We are coming to the end, the turkey has been cooked.*
> Malcolm McLaren

This chapter examines the difficulties of communication in the twenty-first century, exploring such issues as media fragmentation and micro audiences. It also explains how the ability to segment, understand key audiences and then target specific groups can benefit marketing campaigns and the marketing strategies of companies and CSOs.

Perspectives

Mass communication is a relatively new phenomenon. Before improvements in newspaper distribution in the nineteenth century via the railways, those wishing to communicate with the population at large (usually the king or his representatives) had to rely on a slow dissemination of information via the written and spoken word through letters, proclamations and the use of town criers. Quite sophisticated systems, based on military signalling, semaphore towers, for example, were developed to provide emergency point-to-point communications. However, individuals wanting to communicate an idea widely had to use such methods as pamphleteering which is, of course, still used today by political activists. Addresses from the church pulpit also played an important role in the dissemination of information and influenced how people understood what was going on.

Individual communications were revolutionised first in 1840, with the advent of the penny post, and then telegraph communications, which moved from the earlier manual semaphore towers and masts to electrically wired systems. Then in the early twentieth century the telephone grew to have widespread availability.

In the twentieth century the channels open to organisations and individuals wanting to advertise or communicate a particular message or idea proliferated rapidly with the advent of radio and television. A very much larger audience was available to UK advertisers from 1958, with the arrival of commercial television. Commercial radio became available relatively late, in 1973, although illegally-operating pirate radio stations offered advertising in the 1960s.

In the twenty-first century with the huge growth of the Internet, electronic mail and mobile communications, the possibilities of mass interactive communications have exercised organisations keen to reach specific audiences with targeted messages.

Alongside these developments we have seen phenomenal growth in the use and power of computers. One of the most important applications of computing to marketing and, particularly, fundraising, has been in the field of direct mail where a single individual or organisation has the ability to 'write' a letter to hundreds, thousands, and now millions of customers or potential clients in an apparently highly personalised way and, increasingly, use the Internet to speed up delivery and cut costs.

Direct mail

Historically, direct mail has formed a vital part of nearly all large charity fundraising activities. Even though results, especially from cold mailings aimed at recruiting new supporters, continue to decline, more players are entering the market as smaller and smaller organisations seek to build regular predictable sources of voluntary income. (See also the 'Direct marketing and direct mail' box on page 3.)

Direct mail statistics

Figures from the Direct Mail Information Service (DMIS) showed that charity use of direct mail continued to rise in the early 2000s with around 292 million items of direct mail sent to consumers by charities during 2002, which accounted for 7.4% of the overall amount direct mail sent that year. DMIS showed furthermore that direct mail volumes in general increased by more than 130% from 1992 to 2002 (Gray 2003). Fundraising consultant, Tony Elischer, commented in a personal interview in 2002 that the increase was predictable:

> If you look at the number of charities still coming on stream with programmes and the fact that almost everybody recognises the importance of bringing on new recruits, then it's not surprising that the use of direct mail is continuing to rise. It's a reflection of the market becoming tougher and charities having to cover all angles.

As late as 2005 the DMIS was reporting growth in the use of charity direct mail (DMIS 2005). However, through the second half of the decade the use of direct mail had fallen dramatically as the use of email has grown. The Fundraising Standards Board reported that the use of direct mail in charity fundraising fell by 27% between 2009 and 2010. In 2011 this figure increased by 18% but was still lower than the 2009 figure by around 28,000,000 (FRSB 2011, 2012). Nonetheless, it is vital that the data generated from direct mail (and indeed all supporter development routes) needs to be managed effectively. As Dr Peter Flory in a personal interview in 2011 reminded us:

> Communication with supporters generates large volumes of data and it is vital to record it and use it effectively to maximise the benefit to the organisation. This is where so many third sector organisations fall down. They still collect lots of data but do very little with it. The first part is the boring part; capturing data accurately. For, without accurately recorded data, any analysis of it and marketing selections (and resulting communications) then made from it will be a complete waste of time.

As with all media, direct mail can still be used effectively in order to meet the key objectives set out and agreed for it, usually, within the organisation's communications plan. Despite the enormous growth in Internet sales over the last few years, mail order firms continue to derive much of their turnover from mailed catalogue services. The same picture exists for charity trading – traditionally around Christmas gift and card catalogues.

The Internet

While the British Red Cross still, for example, took only a small percentage of its total Christmas sales via the Internet, this was nevertheless an increase over the previous year and is certainly expected to continue growing in importance. Jeremy Hughes (former director of fundraising at the British Red Cross) had a very pragmatic view, however, and commented in a personal interview in 2002: 'The Internet is just another way of reaching people. In response to a major international emergency, it is possible to cut through the noise and attract significant funds. Outside of appeals that enjoy such mass media support, the Internet has not yet proved a serious challenger to more traditional direct marketing techniques.' Indeed this seems to be confirmed by the research organisation nfpSynergy which reported that in the previous 12 months only 3.7% of charity donations had been originated through the Internet (Tracey et al. 2011).

Fundraisers in charities who are charged with developing income streams face very similar problems to their sales counterparts in companies. Investment now has to be spread over an increasingly diverse range of media, including the Internet, as fragmentation gathers pace. It should be noted that the Internet in itself is not a medium but encompasses media – it is the world reflected electronically, so any traditional media such as newspapers, television and radio are mirrored on the web. There are also new media which only exist in the electronic world, including social media such as Twitter. That is not to say that these do not in return become reflected in traditional media; printed newspapers, for example, will often quote tweets.

The potential of the Internet is perhaps illustrated by the growth throughout the 1990s of seasonal charity trading catalogues for spring and sometimes summer both to increase overall sales (or slow their decline) and, perhaps more importantly, to smooth the resulting trading patterns over more of the year. Online catalogues can be updated at far more regular intervals than their paper counterparts without incurring huge print and distribution costs. Indeed an organisation can be very opportunity-orientated by listing and de-listing products or services depending upon news and current events. Many Internet portals such as Google, MSN, Virgin, Yahoo and the BBC respond very quickly to daily or even hourly events, posting links and offers that hook directly into people's interest in the event which may, in reality, be quite peripheral. Aspects of which messages should be communicated to which audiences are covered in more detail in Chapter 8.

In the same way as a multimedia approach needs to be applied to mail order and trading, so fundraisers must consider the varying merits of direct mail and email over other channels, depending upon the desired objectives. Clarity is all-important and realistic expectations need to temper enthusiasm to get the job done.

Thus, for example, the approach to organising an emergency appeal has changed quite dramatically from that which may have been successful ten years ago. A fundraising appeal for an urgent, unexpected activity might then have elicited a 24% response from a database of 220,000 active givers at an average of £21, yielding just over £1.1 million. The costs of that mailing would have been around £110,000 allowing for first-class postage and response handling, which would mean a net £1 million towards the project. Today's fundraisers, however, would need to organise a multimedia campaign to get anywhere close to these results.

Mail could still form the backbone of a fundraising appeal today. However, going to a database of perhaps 250,000 givers would elicit a much lower response rate for two reasons. First, from anecdotal evidence, the overall response to warm, supporter mailing has dropped significantly over this time frame and second, most charities have concentrated upon both recruiting new givers via regular giving methods, and converting existing supporters to similar regular donations. The scope, therefore, for one-off responses to a perceived emergency is much less. The mailing, even with telephone follow-ups, might produce a response of 16%, which would give an average of £21 (excluding regular monthly givers – averages according to CAF changed little between 2007/08 and 2010/11, although there was a statistically significant dip in 2011/12 (Dobbs et al. 2012)). This means a yield of £840,000. However, provided that the organisation has a carefully built-up database of email addresses for supporters, enquirers and site visitors, then Internet site announcements and emails to all known supporters could easily take the gross back to £1 million if 5% of an email campaign to 100,000 addresses yielded £30 each. The costs overall, however, are likely to have increased to £150,000 allowing for the differing channel costs and fragmentation. Thus for increased effort and complexity the net contribution may have fallen by £160,000 over the period. (This is a fictitious example but based on an accurate composite of several real examples.)

As Howard Lake, publisher of *UK Fundraising*, the leading Internet information resource for fundraisers, commented on the significance of digital channels (personal communication 2011):

> Digital communication is now an essential element of any organisation's marketing. It affords flexibility, reach, measurement and impact to any size of organisation. Ten or more years ago lack of money was the barrier to many charities wishing to use direct response television or direct mail, whereas now, with free tools like Twitter, Facebook and email, the only barriers for charities are access to skills and expertise.

A charity's website and email marketing should still be at the heart of its digital marketing activities because those are the assets that it controls. The majority of its campaigns, fundraising and communications efforts will attempt to drive people back to the site to take action. To help them achieve greater impact, charities now have a wide range of third-party services to assist with their digital communications and fundraising. These include eBay for Charity for online trading; JustGiving (and VirginMoney-Giving, BTMyDonate, Bmycharity and others) for online donations and sponsored events; MuchLoved for online tribute giving; easyfundraising.org.uk and Give as you Live for online affiliate shopping; Guess2give for combining sweepstakes and events; WeDidThis for crowdfunding projects; Rapidata Services for regular direct debit processing; Vir2 and JustText-Giving for mobile text giving; and many more. Lake added, 'In addition. charities realise that they need to spend time where their donors spend their time online and that is at social media sites like Facebook, YouTube, Twitter and LinkedIn.'

In fact, given the numbers of people who use Facebook alone and the amount of time they spend there, it is essential for charities to test how they can make the most of these social spaces. The opportunities are extensive, from direct fundraising to securing new givers, conducting market research, integrating with offline fundraising, providing better giver support and greater transparency, and moving rapidly to take advantage of new opportunities. Lake further commented that:

> The real significance to charities of these channels, however, is the fact that they were built to be social and to operate from mobile devices as well as desktop PCs and laptops. As social channels, charities can now benefit from their supporters who have discovered how to use them to support their charity, spreading the message to their networks – networks that the charity could not previously have reached.

> As mobile devices edge closer to becoming the most popular method of accessing digital information, charities are going to find that mobile digital communications are going to offer more possibilities but also greater challenges in terms of managing and exploiting them effectively.

Here Lake is also referring to the fact that as television has gone digital and the distinction between PC, Internet terminal and television blurs, so the need to present coherence will intensify.

Peter Sweatman is the founder and former chief executive of the Charity Technology Trust (CTT). He believes that the Internet can provide far more than direct marketing opportunities and may be one of the avenues through which corporate organisations and charities can begin to work more closely on joint marketing initiatives, as opposed to collaboration, however worthy, on community affairs and issues. CTT was formed as a charity with the aim of helping other CSOs to make much better use of the available technology. Sweatman explained in a personal interview in 2002 that 'the cost of developing a bug-free, secure platform would be prohibitive for any individual charity. We provide a single platform with multiple use and already have raised £70k extra revenue for our partners.' He went on, 'However, this is only the start. The lottery engine is a practical, valuable example of what we can deliver because we have the knowledge, expertise and backing to continue investing and developing other platforms. CTT needs to be considered as the single source for such technology. Ultimately our boiler plates should be free.' By this he means CTT's products will be like other software, where, in the way that first-generation products are expensive, the next generation are produced in higher volume and more cheaply and finally programs and utilities become shareware. This is how he envisaged that CTT would grow and service the needs of many more CSOs.

For all the enormous investment in Internet resources, technology and communications programmes, producing income via these means remains a modest part of total individual income generation for most charities. As noted, nfpSynergy's recent research among participating charities indicated that less than 4% of their income was generated through Internet activity (Tracey et al. 2011).

Mobile phones

CSOs are, of course, always looking for new ways to raise money quickly and easily and many are turning to the boom in mobile phone technology to boost donations. Text messaging or SMSing (Short Messaging Service) is being used to carry broadcast advertising by both network operators and mainstream advertisers that seek to influence the predominantly younger audiences using the technology. Since July 2009 operators agreed that donations are VAT-free (BBC 2009), so charities can consequently mount very low-cost campaigns, typically for £5 gifts, with no network charges, save the 10p text charge. A number of television campaigns are running with a text donation being the prime ask.

A few years earlier, before the networks had generally agreed fee waivers, Comic Relief asked people to sign up to receive messages in the run-up to Sport Relief day. As a result they raised 1% of their £10 million total by SMS. They ran two competitions and 320,000 supporters text messaged or phoned their answers to a premium rate number costing £1, of which 60p went to the charity. 'It was a big success,' said Jackie White in a personal interview in 2002, then media relations manager for Comic Relief. 'We believe this was the first time a UK charity had used SMS to fundraise. It's a very easy way for people to get involved.'

But even with the huge uptake and use of smart phones, text messaging, email and other technologies, they are unlikely to replace other forms of campaigning completely. Ceri Edwards, director of policy at the Institute of Fundraising, said that email and SMS are likely to remain just part of a package of techniques, like direct mail: 'The great thing is that wherever people go they take their mobile so charities can reach them immediately, rather than having to wait for them to go into work to look at their emails', Ceri pointed out. He noted also that 'there is only space to get across a relatively short message using mobile phones to receive email or SMS, so there will continue to be a need for a range of leaflets and support materials '(personal communication 2012).

If all else fails it is possible to make money from unwanted and redundant mobile phones, like used toner and obsolete computers before them. A large number of charities have launched schemes to recycle such equipment for use in the developing world, gaining up to £30 per handset.

Print media

For many years, newspaper and magazine advertising has been the staple recruitment medium for charities and many commercial organisations. As Stephen Pidgeon said in a personal communication (2002), 'print is still alive and well'. In Pidgeon's mind, however, what has altered is the rate of change. He feels that, with direct marketing, budgets for print and mail are being cut in favour of face-to-face recruitment, and charities and agencies have to work harder, faster and smarter to achieve acceptable results.

Pidgeon points to the umbrella campaign, Remember A Charity. In 2000, a consortium of charities came together to launch Remember A Charity, and by 2012 it was working on behalf of more than 140 charities to raise awareness of the benefits of writing a favourite cause into your will. It aims over time to help to increase the percentage of those writing charitable bequests into their wills. When the campaign was founded, 14.3% of wills at probate included a charitable gift, whereas latest available figures from Smee and Ford's notification service show the percentage to have risen to 15.7% (Remember A Charity 2011/Legacy Foresight 2012). The hidden face of the campaign is working to influence financial advisers and will-makers to be much more upfront in asking clients whether they want to help a favourite cause in this way. An example advertisement from the campaign is featured (see figure 7.1), alongside a more conventional charity will advertisement (see figure 7.2). It remains to be seen whether such a campaign, distanced from the very powerful causes it espouses to help, can make any real difference.

FIGURE 7.1 ADVERTISEMENT FROM THE REMEMBER A CHARITY CAMPAIGN

'I should never have switched from Scotch to Martinis'

These were believed to be Humphrey Bogart's last words, but it was his wife, Lauren Bacall, whose words said the final goodbye. In his urn she placed a small gold whistle inscribed: 'If you need anything, just whistle,' the immortal line she delivered to Bogart in 'To Have and Have Not', their first film together. We all have our own way of saying goodbye, but if we all did it by leaving a gift to charity as well as our family in our wills we could make a huge difference. Otherwise, most charities will struggle to survive and that's one farewell the world can do without. **Make your last wishes something to remember.**

REMEMBER A CHARITY IN YOUR WILL
Help the work live on...

Find out more at rememberacharity.org.uk or come and see us at stand 24.

Registered charity England and Wales (no. 1079573) and Scotland (no. SC038971).

FIGURE 7.2 EXAMPLE OF A LEGACY ADVERTISEMENT

BROOKE HOSPITAL FOR ANIMALS
founded in 1934 by Dorothy Brooke

Your legacy will bring good fortune...

...to a hard-working brick kiln donkey in India,
or an ill-treated horse in Egypt.

For almost 70 years, the Brooke Hospital
has been changing lives in the world's
poorest countries. We ease the suffering of
sick and injured working horses, donkeys
and mules with free veterinary treatment.
And we show their owners how good
animal management can benefit them, too.

Our work is enduring, reaching generation after
generation of animal owners. With your support,
we can work together to make a real difference
– for years to come.

So when you are remembering friends and family in your
Will, please consider remembering the Brooke Hospital.
You will bring lasting good fortune to animals in need.

**Brooke Hospital for Animals, Broadmead House
21 Panton Street, London SW1Y 4DR.**
Registered Charity No. 1085760

To speak to our Legacy Manager, please call
020 7968 0807
or email: **legacies@brooke-hospital.org.uk**
for advice or further information.

Your legacy won't just help treat the pain of
overworked donkeys like Basanthi here. It will ensure
that her owner knows how to respect and care for the
animal he depends on – and his children will, too.

Broadcast media

John Logie Baird demonstrated the first television broadcast in 1924 and the BBC made the first public broadcasts (using EMI's rival electronic version) in 1936. However, it was not until the Coronation in 1953 that television-set ownership took off in the UK and began a communications revolution, which is continuing today. In 1958 the first commercial television station opened with an advertisement for Gibbs SR toothpaste and for many years the cost and perceived value of broadcast television advertising dictated that well-established consumer brands were the only regular users of the media.

Radio and television are the mainstays of much fast-moving consumer goods advertising and many larger charities have invested, with varying levels of success, in the use of such media for direct-response advertisements to recruit new givers. What has changed over the last few years is the increasing rate of fragmentation of channels and programming. This means that achieving the task of showing the right advertisement at the right time to the right audience is proving ever more difficult to achieve.

Interactive television has for some time held out the possibility of engaging with the right audience and securing not just orders or donations but an informed response and feedback to issues and campaigns presented. Unfortunately in the UK this had been, until the demise of ITV digital and the launch of the BBC/Sky competitive response, the bailiwick of the satellite and cable operators with, proportionately, very small audiences. Five free-to-view channels became dozens and the potential to build upon this is enormous.

In addition the Internet, with its increasing ability to carry broadband video communications into the home, and the cinema, with an ever increasing number of multiplex, small screen operations, offer additional outlets for sponsored and supported programming by CSOs even if direct advertising remains beyond them on cost grounds. In reality, with small audiences and even more specialist programming, appealing to limited constituencies, advertising and sponsorship rates will fall further in real terms, which may offer opportunities to quite small organisations. However, to contact these small audiences effectively through mobile communications, the Internet, interactive television, cinema and DVD, the organisation

Permission marketing is where a customer gives marketeers permission before they take any steps to send promotional messages to that customer. The aim of it is for people to receive relevant messages which they genuinely want and will not ignore (which is the fate of many unsolicited marketing messages). This approach treats consumers with respect rather than assuming permission just because it may be legal to send messages to any given consumer.

must seek each individual's explicit permission. The whole area of permission marketing where customers choose whether to opt in or opt out with regard to receiving marketing messages continues to be a source of wide debate.

As Phil Nunn, Global Communications Planner at BDF, one of the larger media-buying organisations, said in a personal interview in 2002: 'The challenge is to see how this fragmentation can be capitalised upon. Advertisers who can learn to use permission marketing will lead the way.' Nunn's view is that a more holistic approach will have to evolve because the new generation of consumers not only 'want it now' but also want it more easily and more simply. Audience fragmentation is then, like so many things, both a threat and an opportunity.

Conveying the right message to the right audience

Marketing communications, increasingly referred to as marcoms, is all about getting the right messages to the right audiences in order to achieve overall marketing goals. This includes selecting and applying the appropriate communications tools available, such as direct marketing, promotional selling, public relations and advertising. Yet, however good the intentions are, the implementation of marcoms plans can produce unexpected and sometimes undesired results.

When Gordon Brown as chancellor made sweeping changes to the tax regime surrounding charitable gifts in his 2002 budget, he could hardly have dreamt that in unscrupulous hands his generosity would come back to haunt him. The major changes to Gift Aid are being communicated by charities to their supporters and to the well-disposed via the Giving Campaign (set up to promote greater philanthropy and tax-efficient giving as an NCVO initiative and chaired by Lord Joffe). The campaign has worked on a number of fronts, rebranding Gift Aid with a new logo and a much more public face. Increasing numbers of charitable givers now automatically Gift Aid their donations. According to HM Revenue & Customs, over £1.1 billion was given in Gift Aid in the 2010/11 tax year (Turner 2012). The right message has reached the right audience even with the reduced reclaim rate because of the lower base rate.

However, the double taxation benefit enjoyed by the giver when making a gift of shares to a charity can be used in distinctly less than philanthropic ways. The intention is to allow any giver to make a gift of shares and enjoy both the tax relief on the gift as well as a write-off of any taxable capital gain.

The Independent reported that an entrepreneur saved £112,000 in tax by donating shares to a charity when share dealing was suspended pending a deal (Cope 2002). Nick Leslau, a property specialist, gave £280,000 worth of Knutsford shares to the British Wheelchair Sports Foundation. At the time of the transfer the shares were worth 80p but they later collapsed when trading resumed. The charity held on to the shares worth at the time just over £9,000. The tax benefit was secured under the terms of the gift of shares scheme, which was introduced at the peak of the stock market boom. Mr Leslau's share transfer was legal, but even a change in government has not yet resulted in the government tightening up the rules on charitable share giving.

It may be that donating shares to charity could be popular among venture entrepreneurs. Selling shares could damage investor sentiment in their companies. Donating to a charity would lock in an immediate tax benefit on shares that are highly valued at the time. Also, many entrepreneurs are subject to lock-in arrangements, which bar them from selling shares within a year of their stock market float. However, depending on the wording of the flotation prospectuses, the lock-ins may not cover share donations.

Many have, of course, taken advantage of the scheme in a genuinely philanthropic way. For example, Sir Robin Saxby, chair of the microchip designer Arm Holdings, donated Arm shares worth £330,000 to the University of Liverpool (ARM 2003). In addition, in 2006 Stanley Fink, the chief executive of the hedge fund, Man Group, donated shares worth around £4 million to an unnamed charity (Muspratt 2006). These moves entitle the givers to an income-tax benefit but also help them to avoid the capital gains tax that would be payable if the shares were simply sold and cash given to the charities instead.

The changing face of communication and communicator

The proliferation of television channels and programming and, as a consequence, the emergence of micro-audiences (for example, niche social groups or networks on the Internet which are engaged, interactive communities) is a challenge that marketeers of all persuasions ignore at their peril. Given the active engagement of these audiences (where individuals contribute to the communities with content and commentary, for example), a targeted approach may have a good chance of having an effect because these communities are more likely to take action as a result of the communication. Phil Nunn gave a useful example of how a charity might react: 'The RNLI might, in seeking to promote their own extension of work from solely traditional off-shore work to include high speed inshore inflatables working in estuaries, attempt to appeal to a much younger audience for this new market segment.' He suggests that using permission marketing, capturing enquiries from young Internet surfers, text messages via mobiles and short video clips via Internet portals could allow the charity to focus on real-life adventures, experiences and shared feelings. The overlap with traditional supporters, who respond to direct mail, press and television advertisements, would, in Nunn's opinion, be almost zero and the risk therefore of cannibalisation or confusion would be minimised, while the opportunity to engage new young audiences could be extremely fruitful (personal communication 2002).

This ability to think about audience segmentation is, or should be, already at the heart of giver and customer communications programmes. As referred to in Chapter 2, page 18, segmentation (if only on the lines of giving history: recency, frequency and monetary value) can be taken much further and can be a very good indicator of future behaviour for supporter prospects. Equally, the type of operation and style of communication that an organisation exhibits can affect the way in which it is perceived by its target audiences.

Social enterprises

Social enterprises, referred to in Chapter 1, can cut across conventional boundaries, challenging stereotypes and enabling the participants to achieve what others would regard as impossible. They are usually hybrid organisations that are formed as a direct response to unmet need where conventional structures (public, private and not-for-profit) have failed to overcome the often huge obstacles preventing improvements, social action and change. In this way, the term 'social enterprise' simply describes the purpose of a business rather than being a legal definition. They are able to involve audiences that are seemingly impossible to communicate with, yet, once involved, these target groups can become not only fully engaged but also active participants in the enterprise itself. Social change is usually a strong motivating force but, in contrast to charity work, individual profit can also be actively encouraged.

Andrew Mawson, when speaking at a conference, had some revealing things to say (CAF 2002). He considered that charity is not necessarily a good thing, because it can create a dependency culture in the sector with projects endlessly awaiting their next public-sector grant. He felt that this dependency can dampen an entrepreneurial spirit, encouraging projects to operate 'in the box' of one funding stream rather than look 'out of the box' for integrated solutions to social problems. Mawson stated that he agreed with Liam Black, chief executive of the Furniture Resource Centre – a successful social enterprise in Liverpool – who argues that many in the voluntary sector need weaning off charity and grants in favour of a business response to social problems.

This is coincidentally the aim of the Community Action Network (CAN), a social enterprise of which Mawson was an executive director. Mawson was made a Lord in 2007 for his contributions to social enterprise and community action groups and now operates as a cross-bencher and director of Andrew Mawson Partnerships. The funding environment has changed radically but his views have not.

CAN is a mutual support service for social entrepreneurs working across the UK, and seeks to move traditional charitable projects away from a culture of dependency towards becoming more sustainable social enterprises, where an increasing proportion of the organisation's income comes through trading. Mawson acknowledged at the conference, however, that this is easier to do when making furniture or removing bulky waste products, and more complicated when you get into the area of delivering community care and health services in areas where there is little surplus income.

Social enterprise definition

According to the Department of Business, Innovation and Skills (BIS):

> The government defines a social enterprise as follows: 'a business with primarily social objectives, whose surpluses are principally reinvested for that purpose in the business or community rather than mainly being paid to shareholders or owners'. The number of Social Enterprises was estimated from the Annual Small Business Surveys using the following criteria:

● A business that has mainly social and environmental aims, and . . .

● Does not pay more than 50% of trading profits or surpluses to owners or shareholders, and . . .

● Principally reinvests its surpluses in the business or the community, and . . .

● Generates more than 25% of income from trading goods and services, and . . .

● Has less than 75% of its turnover derived from grants or donations.

BIS 2011

He commented further that he had seen millions of pounds of charitable monies wasted in charities: too many people possess too much ideology and too little know-how about using money in a business-like way. He suggested a more regulated but collaborative way forward that might retain and promote the energy required to communicate and act where both conventional for-profit and not-for-profit organisations would wilt.

This point of view goes way beyond the government's own ideas in terms of changes and regulation for charities, and other social entrepreneurs have a far more pragmatic attitude. David Tootill (2011), the founder of the very successful community interest company (CIC) SouthBank Mosaics, says, 'SouthBank Mosaics exists to help young offenders by offering them a creative, practical outlet and new set of skills. The CIC structure is just the most effective way of allowing the organisation to prosper.'

Doing things differently

Maintaining a coherent message

While, as Oxfam illustrates, a comprehensive approach to marketing is not impossible, it remains very rare. Simon Collings, former director of fundraising, said in a personal interview that the charity needed to complete a full review of the organisation's marketing during 2005, which allowed restructuring and the resulting improvements to be implemented. Collings added, 'We made these changes to put the supporter, not the campaign, at the heart of all our communications and fundraising activity.' This is music to the ears of those who firmly believe that CSOs must take a holistic approach to marketing and ensure that givers, customers and clients receive coherent, welcome messages from the organisation that they have chosen to support or trade with. Oxfam has already gone a long way down the route of having an integrated, coherent marketing approach but, as Collings said, 'Like a lot of modern businesses, we turned away from promoting a range of products and asked ourselves how people want to interact with the Oxfam brand.' He added: 'The crucial element was to change the way people work, to get them thinking beyond the particular operational role they may have and see how this fits into the overall strategy of the organisation.' He concluded:

> Many [fundraising and communications] staff working for charities still don't have marketing backgrounds. We have to ensure staff have a good understanding of supporters and what they are looking for. We also need staff to be constantly making connections with the work of colleagues and looking for opportunities to inspire supporters. This requires a different type of leadership from senior managers who have to act more as creative catalysts and less as traditional managers. Without a change to the internal culture it will be very difficult to achieve our goals.

Maintaining a consistent message

Tony Cram (2001) cites the example of Flora, produced by Unilever subsidiary Van den Bergh Foods. The brand values relate to caring, health and trust and the brand conveys a professional approach to healthy living. Every brand encounter confirms the message. From the first advertisements in 1965: 'Flora puts natural goodness into good eating' to the message in 2000: 'Flora people care', the brand has communicated a consistent core theme. The ongoing sponsorship of the London marathon is totally consistent with the product's healthy identity and the way that the sponsorship is executed each year follows the brand standards precisely. Further promotion with the

British Heart Foundation in 2012 follows similar consistent lines. Pack design is clear, bright and lively and packs carry a care-line telephone number. Call this number and the agents who take the calls are brand champions. They sound professional, helpful and have a high level of expert knowledge. Similarly the website is a valuable source of health information and consistent images. Best practice dictates that every point of contact with the brand must be in keeping with the expectations set.

Reinforcing brand values

Cram's main argument in his book *Customers that Count* (2001) is that organisations must learn to value their best customers and supporters. He reminds us of the old 80/20 rule, the Pareto principle that repeatedly demonstrates that 80% of business is done by 20% of the customers or, more usually, 20% of clients help generate 80% of the profit. Commercial and not-for-profit organisations have to work very hard to ensure those 20% in particular have a special relationship with the organisation. As Flora shows, appropriate investment in working with CSOs can be very necessary to reinforce and maintain brand values.

Yet some of the portents for charities are not good. Even during 2006, before the recession kicked in, large companies were donating less of their profits to charity, reducing their level of giving for the first time in six years, according to published figures from the Directory of Social Change (French 2006). Further figures from the Directory of Social Change show that the top 600 UK companies gave around £762 million in total contributions including £512 million in cash donations in 2009/10, a total of 0.44% of pre-tax profits, which was 0.2% less than the previous year (Lillya 2011).

Cathy Pharoah, Professor at CASS Business School, said at an Institute of Fundraising meeting of the IOF consultants' special interest group in February 2010 that company donations are falling and that at best any increases will be through gifts in kind which can be notoriously difficult to use effectively. She continued saying that companies seem very shy to reveal actually what they are giving in terms of cash and gifts in kind that can be turned into money. In terms of global figures she reported that, for 2008, worldwide corporate investment had increased in 11 of the top 20 corporate givers (though the balance between cash and gifts in kind is far from clear). Worldwide corporate investment of the top 300 corporate givers in 2007/08 moved to a new high of £1.7 billion, but of this some 37% was via product donations from AstraZenica and GlaxoSmithKline. Furthermore, she added that the worldwide corporate investment was only 0.9% of pre-tax profit if product donations were excluded (Pharoah 2010).

Promoting corporate giving

As can be seen from Pharoah's comments, levels of UK corporate giving are in stark contrast to the USA, where there are much greater tax incentives to give to charity. There, corporate donations to charities amount to 2% of GDP compared with 1% in the UK (Pharoah 2008), and this is despite much publicity calling for companies to give more. Out of a total voluntary sector income of £35 billion, only 5.7% came from the private sector (CAF & NCVO 2010). Furthermore, of the companies listed in *The Guide to UK Company Giving* (which reports the vast majority of the corporate giving in the UK) the top 25 companies account for 60% of the total cash contributions (Lillya 2011).

However, not all measures of corporate contributions show quite such a bleak picture. BITC's Per Cent Club was set up to enable companies to demonstrate the totality of social investment, including cash, employees' time, skills and resources, though one of the founding members, Lord Laing, regretted that companies had, as he said at a House of Lords reception in 2001, 'bottled out of it being the one percent club, with only the aspiration remaining' (author's personal attendance). In the USA, by contrast, member companies commit to give 1% of their pre-tax profits.

Business in the Community (whose members are largely plcs) encourages its members to focus on issues in the workplace, marketplace and environment, as well as in the community. Interestingly, in 2007 BITC recognised the Co-operative Bank as the most corporately responsible company in the UK, although, clearly, it a cooperative society.

The challenge then is to find the different ways for commercial and not-for-profit organisations to work more closely, following the examples cited earlier of some companies such as Tesco and Mitie which are beginning to understand the long-term value of effective partnerships.

Conclusion

As Marshall Mcluhan is quoted as saying at the beginning of this chapter, 'The medium is the message', but marketeers have the opportunity to select the media and the message. A mismatch inevitably results in brand confusion, loss of consumer confidence and reduced supporter participation. Congruence leads to increased synergy, a growing reputation and the inspiration of confidence in all participants. Where the organisation cannot adapt, or does not have the right fit, it must take on appropriate partners. That is the marketing challenge.

CHAPTER EIGHT

Reaching your audiences

Never walk away from failure. On the contrary study it carefully and imaginatively for its hidden assets.
Michael Korda

When choosing between two evils, I always like to try the one I've never tried before.
Mae West

The previous chapter looked at the difficulty of communicating via ever fragmenting channels. This chapter examines more closely the various communications methods that are available to marketeers, together with the issues that surround them. It includes a discussion on the use of shock tactics in advertising and the need for real-life stories in the media. Specific use of the Internet and other digital channels is also examined and contrasted and the abiding power of passion is commented upon.

Perspectives

The fragmentation that has occurred in print, broadcast media and through the Internet over the last two decades presents both dangers and opportunities for those seeking to communicate key messages, establish brand identities and elicit support either through sales or donations.

Mobile phone technology has assisted in the proliferation of communications channels firstly with text messaging, then email and then through Wireless Application Protocols we have 'Smart' phones and 'Apps', providing further opportunities to reach highly segmented target audiences. The technology already exists, should the organisations choose to use them, not just for McDonald's to alert customers nearing branches about special offers, but also for Oxfam to tell potential customers that they are approaching one of their 700 retail outlets in the UK.

With the proliferation of digital channels, direct-response television (where people are invited by a television advertising campaign to respond directly to an organisation by making a phone call or going to its website after the advert has aired) has become far more affordable for small to medium-sized CSOs to mount a campaign aimed at key target audiences via the large number of freeview, cable and satellite channels. While audiences may not be large, it is becoming possible to purchase airtime dependent upon response rates. (That is, a cost per response is agreed with the media provider, thus sharing the risk of a poor reaction.)

The growth in local radio stations has fragmented radio audiences further and increased competition for the advertisers' budgets, making it even harder to buy airtime simply by audience figures and demographics alone. Instead media buyers have to consider the acceptability to the audience of a particular message and the context in which it will be received.

For organisations that use direct mail to recruit new givers and elicit continuing funds from existing supporters, the problem is much the same. As the volumes of cold mail increase, existing givers known to be direct-mail-responsive become increasingly alienated by inappropriate charity communications and so responses to cold and warm mailings fall inexorably. The challenge is for the communicating organisation to create better context and greater relevance.

Shock tactics

The use of shock tactics is the strategy of employing shocking images or descriptions in advertising campaigns to grab an audience's attention, elicit outrage and mobilise people into doing something. Amnesty International has in the past made very effective use of photographs of horrendous instruments of torture and examples of violence, alongside the stories of the victims of such atrocities, and continues to have success with challenging and provocative advertisements.

Amnesty's advertising frequently shocks the reader by comparing the ease with which they can join the organisation with the difficulties experienced by Amnesty International members elsewhere in the world.

Figure 8.1 shows an example of the type of challenging image which can be successful. In this instance, however, although the campaign was acclaimed by academics and advertising people, Amnesty was concerned that the images were too graphic and decided not to run the campaign widely.

Appropriateness and relevance

The appropriateness of anything that may shock must be given thorough consideration very early in the planning of the campaign and the ramifications worked through to gain the agreement of all those who may have to respond to criticism and comment. The organisation must be fully aware of the possible impact and be prepared to counter both press comment and individual criticism. Action plans must be produced, likely question-and-answer scenarios developed and, perhaps most important of all, internal communications must ensure that the whole organisation knows why such tactics are being used within a campaign or strategy.

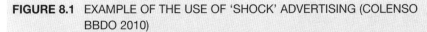

FIGURE 8.1 EXAMPLE OF THE USE OF 'SHOCK' ADVERTISING (COLENSO BBDO 2010)

In the development of giver relationships, many fundraisers are increasingly moving away from negative imagery which may produce a short-term guilt reaction with an accompanying uplift in donations but which has the danger of alienating long-term supporters who become weary of having, as they might feel, their emotions manipulated. Arthritis Care developed a set of guidelines around the question: 'Is it – *positive, honest, powerful* and *urgent*?' with regard to fundraising and awareness advertising, to avoid criticisms by people with arthritis of being turned into victims, sufferers and, as a result of the demeaning stereotypes, incompetent people deserving only pity. By concentrating on positive outcomes the charity was able to square the circle around capturing attention, interest, desire and action without alienating service users. For campaigns that are aimed at mobilising awareness and action from government, say, the organisation used a sense of outrage and injustice about issues of the lack of facilities or resources for the nine million people with arthritis in the UK today. This integrated well with the fundraising strategy and enabled each to support the other.

The use of shock must be equally carefully considered in relation to existing supporters, making sure that they are aware, for example, that a campaign is about to break, why the organisation is using these particular tactics, the expected outcomes and what (if anything) is expected of them. This can go a very long way towards preventing criticism and a negative response arising from important segments of the very audience that has been targeted.

Case study: Barnardo's

Throughout the decade from 2001, Barnardo's shocked the public by running explicit advertisements portraying the victims of child abuse and deprivation and the impact upon the child's later life in terms of suicide, prostitution and drug abuse. Barnardo's denied that the 2002 Stolen Childhood campaign was designed to shock readers gratuitously, but agreed that it did want people to reappraise their attitudes both to Barnardo's – the organisation – and to the issues about which it campaigns and for which it provides services.

The organisation's series, which featured adult faces superimposed upon the bodies of children with the strapline: 'Abuse through prostitution steals children's lives', caused complaints to be made to the Advertising Standards Authority. A spokeswoman for the ASA said: 'People have found the adverts distressing, offensive and unsuitable to be seen by children'. Barnardo's responded that: 'We wanted to make an impact ... but we are not in the arena of shock advertising' (Prasad 2002). Barnardo's had previously courted controversy by running an awareness campaign using a similar age-manipulation device. One advertisement showed a baby injecting heroin. Campaigns from 2005 to 2012 continued to court controversy by featuring challenging issues including child abuse and sexual exploitation, and the organisation's first television campaign, Break the Cycle, was aired in 2008 (Barnardo's 2012).

Interestingly, these sorts of campaigns are nothing new. In fact the founder of Barnardo's, Thomas John Barnardo (1845–1905), initiated the tradition in the nineteenth century. In the 1870s, he started opening homes for orphans and then began, rather adeptly, to make use of images of the rescued children in fundraising advertisements. The adverts would show 'before and after' pictures where recently rescued orphans would be seen first in a state of neglect and then, after having been looked after in the home, looking clean and full of promise. In 1877, however, Barnardo was accused not only of staging the photographs, but also of using the charity's money to his own advantage. In addition, some of Barnardo's accusers felt that the images, in showing the bare limbs of the children, were indecent and provocative. Worst of all were the allegations that children were being physically abused in his homes.

An evangelical Baptist minister named George Reynolds condemned Barnardo's artifice as destroying the 'better feelings' of the children. Barnardo admitted in court in July 1877 that he had indeed taken artistic licence with the photography; however, he stated that he had good reason for doing so:

> We are often compelled to seize the most favourable opportunities of fine weather and the reception of some boy or girl of a less destitute class whose expression of face, form, and general carriage may, if aided by suitable additions or subtractions of clothing, convey a truthful picture of the class of children received in unfavourable weather, whom we could not photograph immediately.

While Barnardo was cleared of most of the charges, the court did condemn his methods as 'morally wrong ... but might, in the absence of very strict control, grow into a system of deception dangerous to the cause on behalf of which it is practised'. Some publicity attempted to reassure the public – *The Times* stated that his homes were 'real and valuable charities, worthy of public confidence and support'.

This was an important case because photography was seen by the Victorians to be a medium which represented the truth. That many of Barnardo's photographs had been staged deeply upset this idea, particularly because these untruths were in relation to innocent children (The Goldonian 2010; Oliver and McDonald 2002).

Nowadays, society is well versed in the tricks of the trade and so there is a higher tolerance for such manipulations of visual media. Government advisor Steve Hilton (previously a partner of prominent social marketing agency Good Business), maintained that manipulating imagery in that Stolen Childhood campaign was legitimate and that it was not a bad thing for Dr Barnardo to have done it in the 1870s. 'That's no longer an interesting debate. What I am interested in is how effective campaigns are in fulfilling their objectives. It is not enough just to raise awareness, they have to achieve a tangible social benefit', he commented. Indeed, if Barnardo were still alive, it would be interesting for him to see the modern images which his charity has been producing. Given that the techniques used also create affecting, yet artificially altered images of children, and for the same good ends, he might well feel justified in his actions – actions which were seen, ultimately, to be visionary (Oliver and McDonald 2002).

Advertising versus editorial

Part of the value of such 'shock' campaigns lies in the amount of 'free' editorial – the comment and reportage that is generated from such controversy. It is often said that editorial coverage is worth several times the value of the equivalent area of advertising. However, this is only true if the message is translated effectively and names or brand identities are as clearly identifiable as they would be in the equivalent advertisement. It is true that a quarter-page editorial is likely to be read by far more of the prospective audience than an equivalent advertisement but again, unless there is clarity, all the effort, in awareness terms, may be wasted.

The difficulty lies, of course, in ensuring that the message, including important identity tags such as names, logos and brand marks, is transmitted through the journalist's desire to make the story interesting, relevant and objective for their target audiences.

An effective example of the use of editorial comment was the Greenpeace campaign against Shell and Esso's plans to dump the North Sea oil rig *Brent Spar* at the bottom of a Norwegian fjord, which utilised a strong reaction of shock in its audience. Even though Greenpeace's technical arguments in favour of dismantling, storing and reprocessing were open to debate, the organisation overwhelmingly won the public relations debate, forcing Shell and Esso to reappraise the entire disposal programme and leading to a complete turnaround in 1995. Similarly BP was forced to drop its 'green credentials' campaign, Beyond Petroleum, when it suffered the disastrous fire and oil leakage in the Gulf of Mexico in 2010.

Real stories – real people

Journalists always want to hear about real people; after all, real people read their reports. For any campaign, suitable case studies of people who are willing and able to be interviewed must be prepared. All too often press releases are prepared with suitable quotations but insufficient preparation to ensure that anyone likely to comment live is able to talk fluently about the issues, including all aspects of branding that need to be communicated. Often the only way to ensure that photographs capture the essence of branding is to use overprinted t-shirts, sweatshirts, banners and other display materials against which people pose or speak. These simple techniques are all too often overlooked in attempts to keep reporters and photographers happy. This has to be weighed against the dangers of exploitation: adopting a 'triumph over tragedy' or 'victims in adversity' angle can create a feeling of simplistic stereotyping which demeans, or worse, detracts from the true story.

Leonard Cheshire's Enabled campaign aimed to persuade more mainstream corporate advertisers to use disabled models in their advertising, not because of or in spite of the fact that they are disabled, but simply because there are 11.2 million disabled people in the UK (5.2 million of whom are adults of working age) who are, therefore, a very significant 'slice of life' (DWP 2011). Part of the earlier campaign was a modelling competition directed at younger disabled people who were keen to become models. This is designed to counter agency and advertiser claims that no suitable disabled models exist. That part of the campaign was successful in gaining media attention because of the human interest stories. Four minutes on the BBC's evening news and a two-page feature in the *London Evening Standard* were a tribute to the work of the charity's media team. The later Creature Discomforts television campaign had similar ambitions around increasing public awareness and challenging existing attitudes towards disability.

However, while these campaigns and messages were well reported, the charity's ownership received virtually no coverage. Does this matter if it helps the campaign achieve its objectives? In absolute terms possibly not, since it could be argued that the campaign is, in effect, the brand. However, within the organisation's overall communications plan is the express objective to challenge public perceptions of the work that the organisation does and help it appeal to a younger audience. Therefore, it could be argued that that news and feature coverage was a missed opportunity. Clearly what the charity could have done was to piggy back on the excellent reportage and to augment that coverage with tactical advertising in the corporate and specialist marketing media, together with further references to the campaign via direct marketing materials or offers, for example.

Budgetary considerations

For smaller CSOs, budget issues are often a further strongly motivating factor. As reported by *The Guardian*, for a team of two working with a very small budget, the Trade Justice Movement (TJM) achieved great success (Gaines 2002). It organised one of the biggest mass lobbies of parliament in history and a survey of MPs revealed that the campaign had had a real impact. The TJM's campaign for fairer international trade was judged the most effective in the biannual charity awareness survey by nfpSynergy, which was part of the Future Foundation at the time. The RNID and the NSPCC with much larger budgets were beaten into second and third place.

Case study: the Trade Justice Movement

The TJM was formed after Oxfam, Friends of the Earth and 40 other voluntary groups, encouraged by the success of the coalition Jubilee 2000 campaign on world debt, decided to campaign for fair trade as a group. It made plans to lobby MPs who, in the eyes of the group, were not aware of their constituents' strong feelings about fair trade. The secret of the campaign's success lay in its comprehensive planning and the group's collective clout. Ms Holt, the TJM's coordinator at the time, commented:

> The crucial time was the five months leading up to the lobby. All the charities in the coalition mobilised their members, asking them to write to their MPs requesting a meeting in June.

> We also met sympathetic MPs who advised setting a tone of co-operation not hostility. We didn't want to attack MPs and stand outside parliament shouting. Instead we gave them plenty of advance warning of the lobby so they could appreciate the issues and have a proper discussion.
>
> Gaines 2002

The TJM coordinated the work of coalition groups and ensured that certain things were done by these groups. For example, each had to send out publicity materials and make sure that speakers were booked for the rallies.

The budget was £65,000 – a very low amount in contrast to other comparable campaigns; for example, £1 million was spent on the Countryside Alliance march. Then Prime Minister, Tony Blair, had originally declined a call for a meeting, but TJM's letter-writing campaign generated so much attention that he changed his mind and met with representatives on the morning of the lobby.

On the day of the lobby, 12,000 people queued all the way from parliament to the South Bank. Holt continued: 'An hour into the lobby I walked along the line and every few yards there was a big cluster of people with their MP in the centre answering questions.'

The TJM tried something new with text messaging, with the idea of raising people's morale while they waited for their MPs. It offered lobbyists the chance to sign up in advance to receive text messages from the TJM on the day. Indeed, when organisers sent on a message of support to the group from then South African president, Thabo Mbeki, lobbyists were delighted.

The total number of MPs (at the time of *The Guardian* report) who had been lobbied was 346 – more than half of the entire parliament (Gaines 2002).

For the most part, the best campaigns use a mixture of placed features, news reportage, paid advertising and direct-response marketing devices. The mix is crucial and should not be rigidly budget-driven, although it is accepted that in many CSOs budgets are inevitably very tight. Remarkable opportunities to buy coverage, however, are often available for tactical advertising if contingency plans have been made.

Ethical questions

Working with a corporate organisation is one obvious way of expanding available budgets, providing that the collaboration is appropriate and does not raise ethical questions. For example, most development charities will not work with Nestle because of its continued inappropriate promotion of dried baby food products (IBFAN 2012). However Shelter, operating with homeless people in the UK, deemed some sponsorship from Nestle to be acceptable (Shelter 2004). But what happens when a commercial organisation seeks the moral high ground? Are charities facing competition from ethical businesses?

'One toy a child will pick up once and never play with again.' This national newspaper advertisement, apparently campaigning against the user of cluster bombs, looks like a traditional charity advertisement. The stark picture, clever headline and powerful text are clearly influenced by years of successful newspaper appeals by the likes of Amnesty International and other campaigning groups.

Yet this advertisement was placed by the Co-operative Bank, with a campaign calling for a freeze on the use of cluster bombs. The advertisement encouraged readers to sign the Bank's online petition or 'make a donation that will go straight towards clearance programmes to help communities return to a normal way of life'. Although it is a large financial mutual organisation, you had to read the small print at the bottom to find that 'for details of how your money will be spent please ask in branch or see our website'. The Bank worked in conjunction with Landmine Action, the 50-strong coalition of voluntary organisations involved with the issue of landmines. It supported the campaign as part of its ethical policy and the advertisements appeared as part of Landmine Action Week in 2002 (Co-operative Bank 2003). So, although the Co-operative Bank is not a typical corporate financial organisation and, as such, it could be seen to be appropriate for it to advertise in this way, it is leading the way for other large financial providers in using shock tactics effectively.

This is not a one-off development. Speaking at a Blackbaud European Conference for Charities in London in 2003, consultant Daryl Upsall warned that commercial organisations could start to take on some of the roles of charities. He suggested that 'it will become harder for the public to distinguish ethical business from charity'.

... And what about sex?

Commercial advertisers have for many years used sex to help sell products and services, and to differentiate brands. The car industry has used scantily clad models to help launch new cars for decades and advertisements featuring alluring actors have been a mainstay of many a manufacturer's promotional programme. Although many accept that this is unacceptable to women, in that it is demeaning and reinforces sexual stereotypes, it still goes on.

Eva Herzigová may no longer be helping to sell Gossard Wonderbras ('Hello Boys') but Lynx continues to use graphic depictions of handsome young men being pursued by scantily clad models and even Lavazza coffee uses erotic fantasy images to help persuade us to buy its product. Sex continues to be used by advertisers to put over images of attractive life-styles, building brand recognition and helping to sell products. So where in all of this are the charities?

It might be thought that the two are mutually exclusive. But are they? The answer has to be a resounding 'yes ... and no'. Passion is a deep, vital element in life and love and its power is there to be harnessed in the service of good causes. Bob Geldof's now infamous passionate plea, 'just give us the fucking money' at the Live Aid concert in 1985 is unforgettable. It is aggressive, powerful and seductive. The Band Aid record that preceded the concert happened because Geldof himself had been watching television scenes of the terrible famine in Ethiopia. He was moved to tears, vowed to do something and the best-selling single *Do they know it's Christmas?* was the direct result. Geldof's passion persuaded dozens of prominent musicians and celebrities to perform, or record messages of support.

However, it is debatable whether sexual passion has a place in most CSO marketing strategies. As advertisers have learned, the brand needs to be seen overtly or by association as being desirable, alluring and sexy. This might work for chocolate and cars but seems improbable for good causes. Nevertheless, without passion it becomes hard to differentiate one children's charity from another or an animal sanctuary from a wildlife conservation trust. Aggression, anger, outrage, desperation are all powerful, appropriate emotions for those seeking to communicate the messages of the organisation. Those can and should evoke passion in the communicator and the recipient. Passion is a vital part of a successful organisation's differentiation and the unique nature of a cause. The call to action must then become irresistible. The call to action through sexual attraction, though extremely potent, can be resisted, however.

Which audience, which message?

Within the planning process decisions need to be made about the desired split between advertising and editorial. In the same way, issues of 'which audience segment needs to receive which part of the message(s)' must be thought through well in advance of the campaign implementation plan, since this will dictate timings and media selection. For example, long-term supporters of a charity, and even potential supporters with the same age profile and demographic background, may well have an existing high level of awareness of the organisation, the cause and the needs involved. The messages within an advertisement placed in *Saga* may be quite different from those destined for the *Big Issue*. The messages within reports or press releases aimed at either audience will also need to have quite different emphases to appeal to the very different audience. One size clearly does not fit all. Segmentation has to be at the heart of these considerations, followed by analysis and agreement to the desired outcomes.

Even where the principal message remains the same, for coherence and impact, then it is likely that different executions of both advertisements and media releases should be considered to gain the maximum exposure and impact. For example, the Symptoms Awareness campaign that was created by the advertising agency Kilmartin-Baker in the early 1990s for the then British Diabetic Association (now Diabetes UK) was enormously successful in both raising awareness of the early symptoms of diabetes (and of the need to visit a doctor if experiencing these symptoms) and helping to double membership over four years. One of the keys to success was the use of differing advertisement executions depending upon the media carrying it: Figure 8.2 shows the generic advertisement, while figure 8.3 shows an example that was aimed at London commuters.

FIGURE 8.2 EXAMPLE OF BDA'S GENERIC ADVERTISING

FIGURE 8.3 EXAMPLE OF BDA'S SEGMENTED ADVERTISING

Is always feeling tired and thirsty, always going to the loo, stopping you from being a City highflyer?

You could be suffering from a form of diabetes. Ask your doctor for a test – diagnosis and simple treatment could quickly restore your old sparkle.

BRITISH DIABETIC ASSOCIATION
10 QUEEN ANNE STREET, LONDON W1M 0BD. REG. CHARITY No. 215199.
A charity helping people with diabetes and supporting diabetes research

For more information
FREEPHONE 0800 60 70 60.

The power of the message

Charities generally have a huge advantage when it comes to developing and communicating brand values. When it comes to changing the world, CSOs can grab the attention. The range is enormous, from Battersea Dogs Home saving and rehoming stray animals to Friends of the Earth, which communicates the idea that it is out to save the planet. The ideas and values must be readily identifiable and in harmony with the mission so that programmes can be developed to communicate them effectively with the organisation's chosen audiences.

In 2002, the Cystic Fibrosis Trust launched an appeal for £15 million, which, if the resulting funded research had been successful, might have seen the charity almost cease to exist within the decade. At that time scientists had estimated that with the appropriate investment a cure for cystic fibrosis might be only five years away. By 2006, £15 million had been raised for gene therapy but the target had risen to £20 million (McKie 2006). In March 2012, with additional funding from the National Institute for Health Research and the Medical Research Council the cystic fibrosis gene therapy clinical trials began. The results of the trial are expected to be announced in spring 2014 (Imperial College London 2012). Breakthroughs that are funded by voluntary income are happening but cures remain tantalizingly out of reach.

Of course most medical research charities have claimed for decades that a cure may be 'just around the corner', and potential supporters may regard such claims as over-optimistic. However, if a new case for support is created and the appeal is communicated effectively, this can produce a very powerful, positive message.

Use of the Internet

The last ten years have seen a further revolution in the way that organisations, especially CSOs, use the Internet and construct websites to assist their communications objectives. First-generation sites were usually no more than digital brochures, describing the organisation and its work. Responses, if invited, were generally via phone or traditional letter. Second-generation sites attempted some interactivity and implemented email links to improve response-handling. They also began to integrate site management into marketing and communications strategies. Now most organisations have learnt that their presence on the Internet is not simply an important part of an effective marketing strategy; crucially, they are beginning to understand that they must consider the audiences viewing it even more carefully than when they create a brochure, mail shot or other publication. Integration of the look, feel and messages broadcast by the site is crucial to avoid inconsistencies and contradictions.

Oxfam has been one of the leading not-for-profit exponents of Internet use. As Andrew Hatton commented in 2001: 'Our website moved from being about Oxfam GB to being Oxfam GB' (Lake 2009). This is an important distinction. First-time visitors get an immediate feel that is certainly replicated in Oxfam's literature and advertising. Navigation is not only simple but also immediately informative, and invitations to join email listings are hard to resist. Permission is actively sought for text messaging to mobile phones and the communication plan to back up such proactive data collection has clearly been carefully developed and implemented.

Howard Lake commented in a personal interview (2011): 'There are still relatively few charities using email really effectively, to communicate. There is an urgent need to build confidence and competence. People must build in-house expertise by getting their hands dirty because Internet product life cycles are getting shorter and the only way to keep abreast is to try it!' His view is that campaigning organisations are learning how to create and use microsites (small websites that are offshoots of their parent websites, aka minisites) to improve campaign reach and effectiveness but that the use of these sites could improve with more effort.

Internal audiences

With the dramatic growth in Internet usage, understanding and ownership are as important for reaching an audience, if not more so, than the implementation of an external communications plan. Where stakeholders buy in to advertising plans and projects, they start with a much better chance of success. Without prior knowledge and understanding, how can staff react to comment and act as brand champions? For charities, the mobilisation of their volunteer network with a united and coherent understanding of the desired communication objectives can be the factor that differentiates success from failure.

Jeremy Prescot, partner at Twentyone Twelve Communications, put it succinctly: 'If internally the objectives are not clearly communicated and understood what earthly chance is there of anyone else understanding the message?' He is quite candid about the role of agencies in helping charities in particular to understand their markets, saying: 'It's up to an agency to do a market audit, without charging the client, in order to really understand the brand' (personal interview 2009). Internal audiences must be considered at an early stage and engaged in challenging ways to ensure consistency.

Overall then, all internal audiences – from the board and management to staff, volunteers and others – need to be as carefully considered as the external ones. These in turn include: existing and potential customers, service users, clients, suppliers, supporters, investors, regulators, policymakers and legislative influencers and indeed any other group or segment that the organisation is interested in communicating with.

Conclusion

In considering the marketeer's audiences and how to reach them, it is vital to analyse the desired outcomes carefully, ensure that they are realistic and achievable and then go about constructing strategies that will deliver the goods.

It is only after conveying an internal message successfully that the same messages can reach chosen external audiences effectively with any realistic chance of achieving organisational objectives. As discussed in Chapter 3, both for-profit and not-for-profit organisations have to consider internal audiences as a vital segment of their target audiences.

CHAPTER NINE

Individuals and organisations

> *You make a living by what you get. You make a life by what you give.*
> Unknown (usually misattributed to Winston Churchill)

> *Donors give blood or body parts; money comes from givers.*
> Peter Maple

This chapter looks at the contribution that individuals make to the process of funding CSOs and considers them not just as givers but also as advocates and champions. In particular, there is some discussion around giving motivation and behaviour, looking at the contribution that a better understanding of these attributes can bring to the marketing process and the way that this can aid more effective fundraising.

Perspectives

Good marketeers know that they have to do careful and thorough research into the demographics of their target audiences. Segmentation by socioeconomic status, location, occupation, pastimes/hobbies, cultural background and age can all be crucial factors in determining possible buyer behaviour.

Good fundraisers know that they have to think along very similar lines about potential givers. One of the most increasingly important, however, is the issue of age. 'Dorothy Donor' or in our case 'Gertrude Giver', the single 80-year-old, is still beloved of charity direct marketeers. But 'Billy Boomer' is the future! In the UK, baby boomers already own 70% of the wealth and this is set to rise to 85% before they shuffle off this mortal coil (Saxton 2010).

Traditionally baby boomers have generally been considered as those born post-Second World War, between about 1945 and 1963. However, there were two booms in birth rates across Europe and America during that period, one peaking in 1948 and one peaking a decade later. Today this second cohort is recognised as being a quite distinct group that is even 'hard wired' differently, and now is classed as 'The Jonesers'. One only has to think of Hillary Clinton (a baby boomer) and Barack Obama (a Joneser) to see that there is merit in considering them as two groups with rather different demographics and behaviour (Pontell 2005).

The generations

Huge resources of time, money, energy and analysis are expended by marketeers in doing demographic profiling in order to understand customers and givers more and segment with greater effectiveness. It is, therefore, somewhat surprising that more effort is not directed towards understanding the very different behaviours, attitudes and beliefs of the different generations. A research study made specific recommendations around this in a report about 30 UK charities and their approach to understanding the potential of major givers (Maple 2009).

Strauss and Howe (1991) developed a generational theory in their work on American society called *The Generations*. In this they tell the history of America as a succession of generational biographies from 1584 to the present. In particular, they wondered why baby boomers and the G.I. generation (people born between 1901 and 1924 in the USA) had developed radically different ways of looking at the world, and whether these generations' growing-up experiences might have prompted these differences. Strauss and Howe also wondered whether any previous generations had acted along similar lines, and their research seemed to indicate clearly that there were indeed historical analogues. They ultimately identified a recurring pattern in Anglo-American history of four generational types, each with a distinct collective persona with a corresponding cycle of four different types of era and mood.

Whether or not these cycles do repeat as they predict, a look at their work does help to provide context and insight into the radically different outlooks and behaviours of differing generations. So, looking at the generally agreed categories of people who are alive today, we have Silents or Seniors, who were born between 1925 and 1942; Baby Boomers, born 1943 to 1960; Generation X, born 1961 to 1981; and Generation Y or the Millennials, who were born between 1982 and 2000. Other demographers (including New Strategist in the US) use slightly different start and end points but generally agree within a year or so of one another. The additional category of Jonesers which was identified by Pontell is particularly useful when thinking specifically about the baby boomers, who are otherwise such a very large, important group for fundraisers and who are becoming increasingly so.

The boomers are coming!

Florence Branchu, a researcher at London South Bank University, conducted some very valuable research into the giving behaviour of different generations as demonstrated through gifts made in their wills.

By 2020, mortality rates in the UK will increase by up to 40%, which could translate directly into more than £1 billion in growth for charitable legacy income if the right actions are taken now. Branchu's research shows that baby boomers are giving differently and, vitally, are writing charitable wills differently. For one really important thing, baby boomers, unlike their parents, know what they are worth (dead or alive). They know the huge differences that have occurred over the last 40 years in property prices (even allowing for recessions) which have affected the value of estates going to probate (Branchu 2011). Fundraising practitioners and charity marketeers are being challenged to respond effectively to these changes in order to grow voluntary income while the baby boomers are still alive.

There is a unique but time-limited opportunity for fundraisers to learn about and understand the giving behaviour and motivation of the baby boomers. Without this understanding and the ability to execute effective marketing, communications and fundraising plans, the potential of a huge growth in voluntary income will be lost forever. Careful consideration will help fundraising practitioners and senior managers to begin to understand the challenge so that they can, in turn, develop an effective response. If further proof of the existing market is needed, Legacy Foresight (2012) showed that legacy income to charities rose between 1988 and 2008 from around £400 million to nearly £2 billion without a significant change in mortality rates. Figure 9.1 shows that baby boomers may still be rocking, but they are about to change legacy marketing forever.

FIGURE 9.1 CLASSIC BABY BOOMERS: 1960S ROCKERS

Addressing individuals

It is not surprising that someone who has had a relation die from cancer or a heart attack will choose related causes when they consider which charities to support with a legacy; health charities do particularly well from legacy income. Personal circumstances matter here more than super hard-hitting campaigns. Longevity and history are also factors; many of today's biggest charities have been around for a long time and that the older generation who grew up with these charities should want to give to them is also not surprising.

Yet in 2009, Oxfam, one of the best known charities, received only £10 million in legacies while Barnardo's, by comparison, received £23 million. On the other hand, by 2012 Oxfam's legacy income was up to £15 million while Barnardo's had fallen to £15 million (as shown in the charities' annual reports). Will that trend continue in the future as the baby boomer generation begin to leave their legacies to a very different mix of charities? There could be a seismic change in charitable donations; they may not reduce in value or volume but they may well go to very different causes from currently. For some charities the doomsday scenario lies in the baby boomers, who may have very different brand preferences and attitudes from those of future generations.

Does anyone believe that people will not begin to leave money to Comic Relief and Children in Need? (Someone has already left a legacy to the Remember A Charity campaign.) Will our development charities, which have often proved to be the most successful and pioneering fundraiser charities from the living, not begin to reap the rewards of legacies, so that Oxfam, Save the Children and others will take the lion's share of such income in the future? The charities that will be successful in this will be those that are asking, not those that are waiting for people to give. Gertrude Giver is dying out and attention must turn, not only to the baby boomers and Jonesers but also to the Daniels, Jasons, Emmas and Sarahs who will be the future givers and legators. Yet for too long supporter databases have failed to allow people to be properly recognised, identified and addressed as individuals. Everyone has purchased broadly similar lists of people to whom to address direct communications.

Technique will drive the method by which people give in the future. Direct mail works for an older generation (the Silents) who like the emotional ask more often than not contained within traditional charity direct mail. However, in an increasingly secular world where belief in organised religion is waning dramatically, could charities adopt an ask appealing to social 'feel-good' factors to replace such belief? It is possible that in the not-too-distant future a majority may no longer believe in an afterlife and instead seek satisfaction in making a difference to this one. Such changes in social priorities now take place over relatively short periods; after all, to the UK population only 30 years ago a holiday abroad was an expensive luxury, the exception rather than the rule. Now it is generally regarded as part of normal family expenditure.

The human race has not changed greatly. Human civilisation emerged out of the necessity to cooperate. It has been in our interests as human beings not to 'walk on by'. Many believe altruism is a basic survival instinct. CSOs today have a marvellous opportunity to fill a gap, a particular need in everyone's psyche to do something worthwhile, to make a real difference, to help change lives for the better.

This need is only ever triggered to any meaningful extent when a charity places before an individual both the opportunity to make a difference and the method by which they can do that, more often than not by making a donation as their pact with hope and a future. So while direct mail and direct-response television may work well with one generation, face-to-face fundraising may be more effective with another.

The spectrum of philanthropy

Philanthropic psychology is an academic discipline which looks at the various and complex motives for giving (Sargeant and Shang 2009). To understand the philanthropic psychology of the baby boomers one must begin to understand philanthropy. There are already a number of existing academic and practical models that aim to describe these motivations and the behaviour of people who give (or, perhaps even more importantly, do not give) to charity.

From early work such as *Why People Give* (Carlson 1968) to the *Seven Faces of Philanthropy* (Prince and File 1994) and *The Selfish Gene* (Dawkins 1976), authors have tended to characterise charitable behaviour as rather fixed. That is, while individuals learn certain altruistic behaviour from parents or society, their subsequent giving tends to mirror a generally learned or inherited response to give in particular ways. For example, Theresa Lloyd (2004) in her excellent book *Why Rich People Give* draws on some hard evidence among a number of very wealthy individuals but then goes on to suggest that these behaviours can be used to predict or at least model the response of other, apparently like-minded, people. This, for the major gift fundraiser or indeed anyone designing an individual giver strategy, can lead to some over-simplified conclusions.

We are all far more 'situational' than most models suggest and, crucially, we are able to move along a 'spectrum of philanthropy' from the most unselfish, genuinely altruistic actions right along to an area of 'enlightened self-interest' (Maple 2008). There is, of course behaviour that is purely self-seeking, under the apparent guise of philanthropy, but the author believes that such behaviour is beyond the visible spectrum of philanthropy, perhaps beyond even the red end of this spectrum (see figure 9.2, which would usually be viewed in full colour) and not a subject to be covered by this iteration of the model.

FIGURE 9.2 THE SPECTRUM OF PHILANTHROPY (MAPLE 2008)

Reciprocity		Enlightened self-interest		Altruism
(BLUE)	(LIGHT BLUE)	(GREEN)	(YELLOW)	(RED)

Altruism

At the one end of the spectrum there are the deeds that seek no reward or acknowledgement. This is typified by the heroic act of a soldier pulling comrades out of a burning tank while being under fire from an enemy. Some may argue that training kicks in but the reality is that there is very little 'benefit' at stake for the soldier and a great deal of risk. Less risky but certainly altruistic was the work of Andrew Carnegie (1835–1919) in the later years of his life. Having amassed a fortune in American iron and steel, he stated that there was nothing inherently wrong in a man making a fortune, but to die rich was to die in disgrace. He spent the last years of his life setting up foundations and disposing of his wealth, giving away the last $20 million in his charitable will (Edge 2003).

Richard Titmuss (1972) in his seminal exploration of the donation of blood, *The Gift Relationship*, looks at attitudes towards public health in the UK where for many years blood has been donated by members of the general public in return for nothing more than a thank you and a small badge when a defined number of donations have been made. He then compares and contrasts with other countries where people are paid for the blood that they donate. Attitudes both specifically to the blood service and to public health in general vary very significantly. Of particular interest to fundraisers is that Titmuss contends that blood donation is an act of altruism or, as he has it, 'creative altruism'.

Yet, Titmuss suggests, there is no one clear definition of an act of altruism. Very different definitions have been ascribed to the term, from unconditional acts of giving, to reciprocal acts, which benefit both giver and receiver. In this instance, however, as represented by figure 9.2, altruism is taken to be at one end of the spectrum of unselfish concern, where gifts are made without any expectation or desire for acknowledgement.

Moving along the spectrum into the area of reciprocity, a large number of people and fundraising activities would be found. Traditionally, charity shops, sales, bazaars, fetes and fairs all offer a tangible benefit to the recipient who can still enjoy a warm glow in the knowledge that the sale proceeds are going totally (or certainly in large part) to the cause organising the activity. From Christmas cards to lotteries and raffles, the purchaser experiences a reciprocal transaction, even though the value of the goods may be trivial in relation to the sum paid.

Reciprocity

The crucial progression along the spectrum is that of movement from no reward whatsoever, through acknowledgement and perhaps 'a little bit of immortality' through prestige and peer admiration to more tangible returns in merchandise, services or the opportunity to win significant prizes.

Throughout the charity world fundraisers are continually thinking up events, concerts, dinners and auctions where people will give and will receive something tangible in return. Fundraising products can be created or modified with a particular audience in mind but, importantly, individuals can move into or out of the target group or catchment and can operate both altruistically and reciprocally. There is unlikely to be equality in the transaction but nevertheless there will be a perception of real value.

At one point along the spectrum, the return to the giver or supporter starts to become as valuable to themselves as to the charity. This is, within this construct, where reciprocity becomes enlightened self-interest. This point, along a variable spectrum, is subject to the participants' perception of the value of the transaction, rather than that of a neutral observer examining the actual monetary or social value of the transaction.

Self-interest

Enlightened self-interest was a concept that Alexis de Tocqueville (1805–1859) discussed in his work *Democracy in America* (1998). The notion he held was that Americans voluntarily join together in associations to further the interests of the group and, thereby, to serve their own interests. Using 'self-interest rightly understood' to describe this concept, he combined the right of association with the virtue to do what was right. This construct takes de Tocqueville's concept further to postulate that in acting philanthropically an important aspect of the transaction may be a strong element of self-interest, even though this may be observed externally as somewhat intangible.

Thus we see people giving freely to cancer research charities both because they are grateful for the benefits resulting to society from advances in treatment but also in the hope that they themselves might benefit from further advances in years to come. Those individuals may move through nearly every one of Prince and File's seven faces of philanthropy as their individual experiences change their perceptions. The different faces are, in a nutshell, the altruist, the devout, the communitarian, the socialite, the dynast, the repayer and the investor (Prince and File 1994).

A more obvious example of enlightened self-interest can be seen in the naming of a new school or other high-profile building after the individual benefactor. The monetary value of the donation may not be perceived by others as worth, say, £3 million (as in the case of an academy where matched funding of up to £20 million is provided by the UK government) but for the individual themselves the 'immortality' achieved is well worth the cost.

Harnessing inspiration

The corporate sector is increasingly trying to gain ground by borrowing the social agenda; witness Shell advertisements on protecting the environment or others in the field of technology that show developing countries making use of the technology to communicate. The message is quite clear. The corporate sector is beginning to learn that a social agenda and the ability to motivate and inspire consumers to think differently is a sure-fire way to enhance brand reputations.

CSOs have nothing to be shy of in this arena. It is vital that fundraisers are never afraid to ask. The individual who has been asked appropriately to support a cause may well experience that wonderful feeling of having done something special. The art of great fundraising is to use the technique that first elicits attention, then produces some kind of action and, finally, slowly but surely, inspires that individual or organisation to believe as strongly as the charity does in its ultimate mission. For charities to change hearts and minds they must be forever stretching the boundaries of credibility and possibility. They must treat everyone as an individual and tailor requests and offers to that individual's keenest desires, while never losing sight of the fact that the driving force behind a charity's mission is the needs and interests of its beneficiaries, not its givers, however important their gifts are.

The following case study demonstrates just how important communicating the case for support is and how, with good planning, passionate support can be retained even when things change shape rather drastically. The crux of the case study is that major supporters were consulted, listened to and treated as individuals throughout the whole debacle. As a result, the outcomes were positive and inspiration was rewarded.

Case study: Crisis UK – modifying giver support when change is enforced

In 2007, at the time the author was Appeals Director at the charity, Crisis UK was faced with some hugely difficult decisions about its major gift prospects. The original plan was to raise £60 million to transform the delivery of services for homeless people in East London by replicating in Tower Hamlets the enormously successful US model known as Common Ground. Unfortunately, however, the appeal and the project, entitled Urban Village, failed through a combination of political weakness and planning naivety. Although the plans were originally recommended by the local council, in September 2006 the application was turned down, following massive pressure from local residents. Crisis made steps to appeal against the decision but, owing to the potential costs and loss of goodwill, was eventually forced to withdraw its plans. The fundraising itself had been successful, securing promises, pledges and cash that came close to the total amount required. Whilst government and institutional funders could simply be released from their commitments, the question remained, what to do with the individual pledges?

In response to this setback, a strategy was created to take account of the overwhelming desire of the supporters (many of whom were indeed baby boomers) to make things better by investing significant sums. A social investment vehicle was developed and launched as if it were a share offering, but returning, instead of cash dividends, a social return on investment (SROI). Urban Investors were asked to join an investment club and receive regular reports of progress. So, while the Urban Village failed, the Urban Investors have helped to fund additional Crisis learning and outreach centres in Oxford, Birmingham, Newcastle, Edinburgh and Merseyside.

In a personal interview in 2011, Mark Astarita (chair of the Institute of Fundraising) commented that the hallmark of most givers' actions is that of 'giving and forgetting'. They give when they're asked and they don't necessarily want a long and beautiful relationship with any one charity. Many enjoy the fact that a number of small donations makes them feel a lot better, believing that they are making a difference to many and varied causes. Astarita feels, therefore, that marketeers must concentrate their firepower, effort and attention on those most likely to give for *whatever* reason. In this case too, inspiration and a determination to share the passion are the key. The brand values of a charity are only as valuable as the effort put in by everyone concerned, from frontline staff to fundraisers and trustees, from the volunteer in the shop to the receptionist on the front counter. They must all smile a welcoming smile and show a passionate belief in what they are doing. Those charities displaying this behaviour may be the leaders in 2020 and their beneficiaries the winners.

Tony Manwaring, chief executive of Tomorrows Company and former chief executive at Scope, said:

> We have come to terms with the short-term thinking and silo deci-sion-making which did so much to cause the financial crisis. Corporate reporting must also come to terms with these challenges, to make the step-change needed so that it is fit for purpose during the global recovery and beyond.
>
> To be effective, reporting must provide more than an integrated account of what is material, drawing on financial and non-financial data. Tomorrow's corporate reporting must fully reflect the needs of the whole system of which it is part and all the key players and insti-tutions who bring the system to life.
>
> CIMA 2011

In a personal interview in 2002 he also said:

> Charities are at their best when they create a bridge between past, present and future; giving life to the values of those who were moved to set them up, providing a vehicle by which their mission can be achieved in today's society, while offering a message of hope and a model for transformation. In this, fundraising and marketing are inextricably linked.
>
> Fundraising is more than about money. It is also the currency of people's desire to make a difference, to make the world a better place. And marketing – at its best – provides the toolkit for a common language which gives that hope form, moving hearts as well as minds. Together, they provide the lever that can enable charities to give people a glimpse of a better future – and thereby to create tomorrow, today.

Encouraging the legacy

The legacy campaign, Remember A Charity, has the objective of increasing the percentage of those remembering a favourite charity in their wills. The number of charitable bequests has risen over the years (as noted in Chapter 7, the percentage of wills at probate which included a charitable gift had risen to 15.7% in 2011 from 14.3% in 2000). The campaign appears to be making some ground and, of course, only time will tell how much progress can be made. There are some positive indications for the future, however. The charity's consumer tracking, which monitors how many people would positively consider leaving a charitable bequest, showed an increase from

11% in 2010 to 18% in 2011. This was the highest level recorded since the charity launched its social marketing campaign (Remember A Charity 2011).

The original consortium grew out of a challenge by George Smith (then chair of advertising agency Smith Bundy) to the fundraising directors of 20 or so larger charities at a private meeting in 1994 of the Appeals Directors Group at the Institute of Fundraising Convention (which the author attended). He said: 'If around a third of the UK population give regularly to charity and less than half of them mention you in their wills then you've got a problem with the legacy as a fundraising product!' He went on to add that as an advertising man he would advocate a major campaign initiative to challenge people's perceptions of legacy bequests, educate those making wills and persuade more of them to write in favourite causes. He challenged those fundraising directors to find the ways and means to address what all agreed was a crucial funding question for the sector.

The group worked on the challenge for some considerable time, trying to conduct research and gain widespread agreement to some form of coordinated campaign. The result was the legacy campaign, the public face of which became Remember A Charity. If the campaign can encourage a further 4% of the UK population to leave a legacy, it could raise £1 billion more each year that could be made available to charities for their core and development needs (Remember A Charity 2011). This, of course, is predicated upon a successful appeal to the very people who are usually resistant to 'charity appeals' and for whom, a vision – the possibility of the world being a better place sometime in the distant future – is absolutely vital. It is vital because baby boomers (the self-obsessed generation) are rarely willing to contemplate their own mortality (Beckett 2010).

Conclusion

It is often said that companies do not give money away, people do. This chapter has looked at the increasing capacity of the current generation of baby boomers to give and examined something of their propensity actually to do so. The attitudes and behaviour of these social investors will have a significant impact upon the ways that charities are able to operate.

This in turn, if executed skilfully, may lead to many more established charities (the best-known and trusted are the ones most likely to benefit from generic campaigns) branching out into new areas, perhaps in partnership with local and central government to cover areas that are currently provided by the state. Distribution of any significant increases in government funding is not likely to be even and could, perhaps, lead to more aggressive takeovers rather than mergers with other charities which are struggling with financial survival. However, the Charity Commission, which is also a victim of cuts, might need to adopt a far more proactive role in allowing such amalgamations to occur.

CHAPTER TEN

The future of social marketing

The best way to predict the future is to invent it.
Dr Alan Kay

Be the change you want to see in the world.
Mahatma Gandhi

In the last edition of this book the question was asked: how might CSOs be operating by 2020? And, even more importantly, how will CSOs rise to meet the marketing challenges of the next decade? In this new edition there is not only an update of the visions of several leading sector figures but also the inclusion of some useful academic insights to provide alternative answers or, at the very least, to offer a provocative picture of the possibilities for the next two decades.

Perspectives

The government's Strategy Unit closed consultation on the *Giving White Paper* in July 2011. While the report is a consultative document, as a result of it indications of the shape of things to come became clearer. Questions remain as to how much of the report will be acted upon and how many of the substantive recommendations will have the necessary legislation, or regulatory powers enabled, in order for them to become a reality. Charities are, for example, still desperate for clarification of the issues relating to street collections in order to address concerns over public confidence. The introduction of giving at cash points, as outlined in the *Giving White Paper One Year On*, while welcome is, in comparison to other issues, trivial.

Whilst the year 2020 seems close in terms of planning time frames, in political terms it will fall close to the possible end of the coalition government's second term, or at the end of a new government's first term which could result in far-reaching changes in policy and practice. Some thoughts about forecasting, therefore, seem appropriate.

Forecasting the future

Bruce Lloyd (Emeritus Professor of Strategic Management at London South Bank University) said in a personal interview in 2011 that 'in the end, all our decisions are taken on the basis of the assumptions we make about the future. Yet, it can be said with considerable confidence that most – if not all – organisations could improve the reliability of their forecasts of the future. The constraint is, invariably, at what cost?'

Lloyd posed two questions which always need to be explored when forecasting the future. The first question is: why do we want to know about the future? The simple answer is usually in order to make 'better' decisions today. But 'better' for whom? It is either for everyone, where the relevant information is essentially open to all; or the other possibility is that one person attempts to take a 'better' view of the future than someone else, as is the case in competitive market situations, where the secret of success is often one person knowing something about the future that the other person doesn't, without abusing the rules relating to the use of insider information. It is also worth bearing in mind that it is not necessary to know everything about the future. Would fans be so keen to watch sports games if the result were known in advance? The lottery would cease to exist. And probably Bernard Shaw's comment 'Most civilizations die of boredom' would apply individually as well as collectively.

But the second question is: can we know the future? The simple answer is, of course, we cannot. But there are some things that can be forecast more accurately than others. Today it can be accurately predicted as to when the sun will rise on (say) 1 June 2050, at a particular point in the world; but, even for a place such as Saudi Arabia, a weather forecast today for the same date would be much less accurate or reliable. All forecasts about the future are, essentially, probabilities and, even with the sunrise example, one can never pretend to be *absolutely* confident in the forecast. Wherever possible, then, forecasts need to be accompanied by estimates of their confidence limits.

Lloyd stated that in essence, therefore, forecasters all try to improve information about the probabilities of what may, or may not, happen in the future, in order to enhance the quality of today's decision-making.

According to Lloyd and Clayton, the most important future-related questions that CSOs must ask in the first place have to include the following:

• What are the future trends and new developments that could have a profound impact on the future business?

• What are the strengths of the organisations, and how do they relate to future opportunities?

• Where could gains be made by early market entry advantage?

• What are the main threats to be faced in five or ten or fifteen years' time?

- Who are the main competitors and what are their strengths and weaknesses?

- Where does prime organisational responsibility lie for exploring options for long-term profitability?

- Is everyone encouraged to share ideas for new products, services and campaigns?

- Is enough time allocated to following up ideas about future opportunities?

- Are senior managers and trustees sufficiently focused on the needs of the future, rather than being preoccupied with legacies of the past?

Adapted from Lloyd and Clayton 2002

Once a decision has been agreed about what needs to be known and why, it is possible to forecast the future more effectively by addressing three key basic process issues.

1. To ensure that the focus is on asking – and trying to answer – the critical questions.

2. To ensure that there is a systematic collection, and review, of relevant information about the future, in order that it is embedded into effective strategy and organisational learning.

3. To encourage greater awareness of sources of information on forecasting the future, which includes relevant websites.

Finally, Lloyd reminded us that 'we should always remember that the quality of the collection, and the effectiveness of the use of that information about the future decisions, depends more on the quality of the dialogue/conversations that are held by all concerned, than anything else. This is where our "better" future begins and ends' (personal communication 2011).

The academic view of social enterprise

Professor Alex Murdock is head of the Centre for Government and Charity Management at London South Bank University and has a particular take on social enterprise. In his chapter 'Social Enterprise' in *The International Encyclopedia of Civil Society*, he notes that:

> Social enterprise as a concept reaches back well beyond the coining of the formal definition. In the UK the early activities of the Salvation Army would certainly have fulfilled the definitional criteria. The

Salvation Army operated commercial enterprises for a social purpose and, significantly, once the social purpose was achieved then did not continue to operate them on purely commercial grounds. Similarly, Alter cites the co-operative movement was very much in keeping with the precepts of social enterprise [Alter n.d.].

Murdock 2010

The first use of a formal definition has been identified as coming from Leeds in the 1979 edition of Freer Spreckley's *Social Audit Toolkit* (Ridley-Duff and Bull 2011). Elsewhere in Europe, as Murdock states, 'the emergence of the concept around that time in Italy [is seen] as having associations with the co-operative movement. Italy was an early developer of a co-operative law which recognised this new form of trading entity (Nyssens 2006).'

With the future in mind, Murdock continues, stating that the rather messy definitional landscape of social enterprise and social entrepreneurship is likely to continue. This is, in part, due to the varying national and cultural landscapes which can be found even in the same country. He says that the research challenges, and therefore directions, can be summarised as being:

- **governance**, particularly in terms of competing *stewardship-* and *stakeholder*-based approaches;

- **financing**, particularly the challenges that social enterprises face in accessing funding and their need for new forms of capital;

- factors associated with **measuring** social enterprise success;

- **relationships with the public sector**, especially in the UK and in some European countries where a similar policy focus has moved towards contracting out public services to CSOs and commercial organisations;

- the need for **external business support services** for social enterprise;

- **marketing**, particularly some of the difficulties social enterprises tend to have in marketing relating to their understanding of pricing dynamics and the need to be competitive in packaging and labelling quality and in providing information for customers;

- **human resource management**, particularly the challenge of managing organisations that are typically staffed by a blend of volunteers and paid workers.

adapted from Murdock 2010

Rangan, Leonard and McDonald have three alternative scenarios (other than maintenance of the status quo) which they believe, with good reason, will make an impact on most of the social enterprise developments in the next decade:

1. Consolidation: In this scenario, funding will keep growing in a gradual, linear fashion and organizations will compete for resources by demonstrating performance, with a focus on efficiency. The sector will consolidate, with some efficient organizations gaining scale, some merging and then growing, and some failing to achieve either scale or efficiency and eventually shutting down.

2. Entrepreneurial: In a more optimistic future, existing and new enterprises will apply strategies to achieve and demonstrate performance, improving efficiency and effectiveness and attracting new funding sources. More organizations will enter a reformed, competitive field of social change with new entrepreneurial models, established traditional organizations, and innovative funding strategies fueling widespread success.

3. Expressive: Rather than focusing exclusively on performance, funders and organizations may view their investment as an expressive civic activity. As much value is placed on participating in a cause as on employing concrete measures of impact or efficiency. In this scenario, funding will flow as social entrepreneurs experiment with new models based on a range of individual priorities and relationships.

Rangan, Leonard and McDonald 2008

The government's view

The coalition government has been, like many before, very strong on rhetoric and less clear on policies that might help the sector. Some would say that it is displaying cognitive dissonance. That is, while talking grandly about Big Society and the value of CSOs, it is slashing spending by central and local government both on commissioned services and grant assistance to community groups and enterprises that are working for social benefit. An NCVO report (Kane and Allen 2011) indicates that the cuts will hit the sector by £3 billion, while London South Bank University estimates the impact to be closer to £5 billion (Maple 2011).

Lord Filkin, the government minister for the voluntary sector in 2002, pointed out that between 1997 and 2002 there was a significant expansion of the private sector in the delivery of publicly funded services (Hill 2002). This change was mirrored in the following seven years, but what will happen now that such swingeing cuts are taking place?

The opposition view

As reported by *Third Sector*, Tessa Jowell, shadow Cabinet Office minister (2010–2012), said that a future Labour government would expect those who use public services to 'give something back' in the form of community activities or volunteering. Additionally, she stated that rewards should be given to volunteers, noting an existing example of Lambeth Council in south London, which gives tax credits to residents who take part in community work.

The article notes that critics have asked why people should be asked to contribute to public services beyond their taxes funding them. Furthermore, sector leaders have pointed out that vulnerable groups, such as disabled people, immigrants and those with learning difficulties, face considerable barriers to volunteering.

Roberta Blackman-Woods, Shadow Civil Society Minister (2010–2011), is reported to have told charities that the next phase of Labour's policy review on civil society would concentrate on social enterprise, social finance and finding ways to encourage banks to support the voluntary sector. She said that the Big Society agenda may work in 'a twee village somewhere' but that it does not address the problems of deprived areas having fewer volunteers. She noted that government must play a role in making sure that voluntary and community work targets the areas where it is needed (Wiggins 2011).

'High tech, high touch'

In a quite prescient personal interview in 2002 Tony Cram, executive educator at Ashridge Business School, had some intriguing suggestions, emphasising that 'ethics are for real!' In other words, companies can no longer hide behind bland statements of corporate social responsibility. His view is that while many corporate organisations have been investing in social auditing and improved environmental impact assessments, the next few years will see a much greater emphasis on operating, and being seen to operate, ethically. This, he said, 'will be a real challenge and an opportunity for charities to work alongside companies, helping to develop and implement some of those programmes'. Cram also suggested that changes in the regulatory regime may be more wide-reaching than many commentators predict. He feels, for example, that trustees will have the same pressures upon them as non-executive directors have today.

With the continuing growth in technology and technical solutions to problems, marketing or otherwise, Cram suggested that the challenge for all organisations will be to embrace a culture of 'high tech, and high touch'. By this he means that while more technology is used to run systems and administer marketing programmes, the winners will be those who are able to keep close to customers and clients. This is the 'high touch' or, as

Every time a customer or supporter has any sort of contact – whether through advertising, editorial content, passive observation, active conversation, the Internet, by telephone, at the cinema, or on video and DVD – with an organisation by seeing, hearing, or conversing about its brand, this is a **touch point** and an opportunity to impress, bore or actively discourage.

Ken Burnett (1996b) suggests in the title of his book *Friends for Life: Relationship Fundraising in Practice*, ensuring that audiences can get as close to the organisation with which they are dealing as they want. Burnett suggests that those who rely on technology alone will be the losers: 'If we allow technology to come *between* us and the donor then its benefits will be temporary and superficial'. This is particularly the case nowadays because there are increasingly more 'touch points', and so it is becoming much harder to manage images and reputations. CSOs, especially charities because of their strong link with supporters, will have to think through their approach to integrating communications much more rigorously to avoid dissonance between all the various touch points.

Cram had a final challenge for companies and charities to work more profitably together:

> With the increasing global view of markets it is not just international charities which will need to form international alliances. There will be opportunities for effectively local or UK-only not-for-profit organisations to work with European and even world-wide partners, to deliver real local benefits in the markets that a global company is seeking to operate and grow.

He added, however, that 'charities will have to seek out talent and communicate much more effectively. Where there is scarcity, salaries grow disproportionately. Perhaps alternative creative solutions will come from the voluntary sector, since collaborations based on addressing issues of mutual self-interest are always likely to be more effective.'

The shape of things to come

Simon Burne, Senior Consultant at THINK Consulting Solutions and a former chair of the Institute of Fundraising, commented in a personal interview in 2002 that 'forecasting ten years into the future is likely to be about as useful as unravelling the pronouncements of the oracle at Delphi or peering at sheep's entrails was to the ancient Greeks'. But he added that 'it's also pretty safe: I'd be surprised if anyone comes back to me in ten years and tells me I got it all wrong!' Ten years on, and much of what Burne predicted has indeed happened or is still happening.

He stated that the public is moving from supporting charities to supporting causes and this has enormous implications for charities. There will be increasing pressure on charities to form coalitions or to merge so that charity equals cause, and indeed cause marketing will take over from charity marketing. Strategy Unit proposals, he said, will make this easier. We will see virtual charities – those existing only in name to channel resources to their member organisations.

As we have seen in this new edition, the appetite for mergers has become a reality and we can expect them to happen more often. The Strategy Unit was based in the Cabinet Office from 2002 to 2010. It carried out a review of the law and regulation of charities and other not-for-profit organisations, which led to the creation of the Charities Act 2006. Based on the review's recommendations, published in *Private Action, Public Benefit* in 2002, the Charities Act 2006 included some provisions to make it easier for charities that would like to merge. Some problems regarding the complexity of merger law have been reported by those in the sector but may be 'marginal' according to a review of the 2006 Act by the Cabinet Office (2012). The review makes some recommendations to resolve the issues, so it will be interesting to see whether these are ironed out over the next decade.

Burne went on to say that causes and issues will rise and fall in the public consciousness increasingly fast, as the media become ever more central to forming public opinion. Cause marketing, therefore, will have to become very much more fleet of foot to capture the hearts and minds of existing and potential supporters. A decade later, and we've already seen the rise in awareness and funding of cause-related consortia and umbrella organisations such as Remember a Charity and the Disasters Emergency Committee.

Linked to this public fickleness, he stated, will be the increasing ease and confidence with which the public can start and stop payments to charities. Traditional customer care may well not be enough in the future and charities will have to explore new ways to develop loyalty marketing. At the same time, there is no doubt that regulation will continue to increase. Charity marketing methods will become more subject to scrutiny and monitoring which may restrict innovation and will almost certainly push up costs.

Ten years on and whilst regulation and monitoring are on the increase, it is largely with more positive consequences than predicted. For example, there has been an increase in data protection regulations resulting in better protection for consumers generally; similarly, the PFRA's regulations which came into effect in 2012 may restrict what street fundraisers can do, but are expected to help improve public confidence in the practice, even though the new rules make fundraising more complex (BBC 2012). With regard to monitoring, charities are increasingly expected, for example, to show their marketing activities' return on investment, which has had a positive effect of demonstrating which techniques are cost-effective compared with those that are less so.

The number of marketing channels for both awareness-raising and fundraising will continue to explode with individual channels rising and falling more rapidly than ever. There will be a great increase in community channels on radio and digital television. With this rise, there will be a segmentation of markets to the extent where mass audiences become a thing of the past. This has advantages as long as charities can identify their segments clearly. There is, however, no doubt that the communications mix will become an even more complicated cocktail. Traditional supporters may fade away and engaged baby-boomer social investors may be the order of the day, for example. In 2013 some of these changes can be observed but rather more slowly than Burne predicted.

He went on to say that successful marketeers will need to develop ways to reach out to and retain new supporters. Face-to-face fundraising has led the way in reaching out to new supporters and will continue to do so, but more marketing will take place over the mobile telephone and, of course, on the Internet. New fundraising products will be offered to these new supporters – perhaps something to replace international challenge events that are in decline. Similarly, ten years later, these trends continue and marketeers who recognise and act upon them are finding success.

Finally, according to Burne, the winners in all of this will be those local charities that possess a strong local presence, and national and international charities which have a clearly defined cause-related brand and high levels of brand recognition. The losers, as is becoming apparent a decade after this prediction, will be the medium-sized national or international charities that fail to merge or join coalitions and causes that do not match the public agenda.

What won't change

In a further decade on from now, the objective of communicating effectively with an organisation's chosen audiences will remain vital, and people will continue to occupy most marketeers' attention. Customer relationship marketing (see page 12) systems may become a great deal more refined and, as Tony Cram postulated in a personal interview in 2009, charities and corporate organisations will probably spend far more of their time and energy cultivating relationships with the top 20% of customers and supporters. Some of the techniques may change to allow greater analysis and the refinement of customer profiling, but the basic practices remain as effective today as they were in 2000 or will be in the 2020s. People give to people. Customers buy and, given half a chance, will continue to buy from sales staff.

The analogue television system wasn't turned off by 2010 but it was in 2012. Many consumers, of course, have simply invested in set-top decoders. The integration of PCs and televisions still has a long way to go but, even when it has come about, it will still be the people watching who make the decisions whether to purchase or not.

A provocative picture

The pace of real change, even taking technology into account, is often far slower than we think (or hope) it will be. How much did UK society actually change in the ten years between 2000 and 2010? How much did the regulatory framework change? It is true that the government changed from the Thatcher years of 1979 to 1990 to a New Labour government in 1997 but many observed that New Labour continued Conservative economic policy over the first three years. Many also believe that they continued these policies into their second and third terms. At the Labour Party conference in 2011 it was admitted that they used the voluntary sector as an arm of government in terms of service delivery. A year earlier saw the first coalition government for more than 65 years take office with a fiscal regime that determined to cut the huge budget deficit whatever the impact upon society.

With that huge growth in CSO income through commissioned services during the first ten years of the Labour government, the sector provided more services and received more of its infrastructure costs in return. There was a rapid growth of the existing major players such as Barnardo's, Action for Children and NSPCC in the field of childcare, RNIB, Action on Hearing Loss, Scope, Leonard Cheshire Disability and Mencap working with disabled people, plus Age UK and the British Legion, together with large commercial providers, working with the elderly. Mergers, large and small, have been happening and now, with huge reductions in local and central government spending, the die is cast. In a not dissimilar way, as noted in Chapter 1, universities and other higher education institutes are also looking for mergers in order to compete more successfully for the remaining reduced central funding.

Consumer-centric communications

Recent research (Roberts and Barker 2010) has identified a shift in society from the passive consumer who over-relied on the voice of authority to a desire to be heard, take more control and become more significant. Feelings of societal emptiness, with little confidence in governments and big businesses, have led to an increasing distrust and lack of interest in brands and have created a consumer desire for a more humanised approach.

The use of digital platforms enables consumers to find trustworthy sources, listen to human voices, express themselves and share experiences. This shift in behaviour has resulted in empowered online communities who own digital space. The influence of people on other people cannot be underestimated, particularly during their purchase decision process. Consumers are increasingly searching for other consumer brand-experiences before making a decision to purchase. Roberts and Barker noted a PR consultant they interviewed who labelled those who provide opinions and content online as 'sharers' and those who read and make decisions based on such content as 'listeners' or 'learners'. Listeners are much more likely to be influenced and persuaded by reports of brand-experiences that are created by sharers because sharers are deemed more trustworthy and genuine than traditional advertising messages.

Roberts and Barker's findings also confirm that if companies wish to survive and operate effectively in the digital space-engulfed twenty-first century, they must understand the new rules of consumer-centric communications. Panellists from advertising agencies, principals of leading digital and social media agencies and marketing directors of B2B – business to business – and B2C – business to consumer – organisations have reported that the 'average brand manager has no power' and is frustrated by senior management, the CEO's resistance to change and lack of digital marketing knowledge. Until senior managers are despatched off to the potting shed (or begin to understand this paradigm shift), little will change.

Consumer-centric communications are, therefore, about being transparent, engaging, and listening to consumers and upholding brand values. If they are not upheld, marketing communicators should genuinely apologise for mistakes and then act quickly to keep their promises.

Consumer-centric communications can be embraced. This, however, requires a long-term strategy and commitment to digital space, despite some inherent risks. Consumers are forgiving if they see evidence of change and human humility in response to their comments and complaints, but if organisations' actions simply pay lip service to any given problem, consumers react negatively. They will discuss poor brand behaviour among themselves on social network sites, blogs, hate sites and demonstrate this via user-generated content platforms. These types of conversations are completely uncontrollable and can damage brand equity and threaten its survival. One has only to look at Trip Advisor to see the havoc that complaints, vexatious or true, can wreak.

When brand values are upheld, however, brand-loyal consumers will look to a two-way online horizontal relationship, one in which they share ownership of the brand with the organisation. Aside from maintaining or repairing relationships through digital two-way communication, further benefits were identified by the panel, such as:

• using feedback to make product improvements, encourage organisational creativity and exercise damage control;

• gaining benefits from having a developed relationship with customers, such as customer leniency and having the benefit of the doubt when something goes wrong;

- creating trust between the consumer and the organisation, and winning hearts and minds;

- making use of positive electronic word of mouth (e-WOM).

All of which leads to consumer advocacy, loyalty and preference for the brand. For receptive and proactive brands, the fact that consumers are sharing information and feedback via eWOM to each other creates an instantaneous 24/7 feedback service, which provides an invaluable research facility.

Unfortunately, however, very few organisations are fully and effectively involved in digital space yet. Just having a presence does not constitute building relationships, trust or nurturing a two-way conversation for the benefit of both parties. Since the greatest contributors to charity funds (via the Internet) are in the 25 to 44 age group (Dobbs et al. 2011) and the same consumers are also prolific users of social network sites, it would be folly not to embrace consumer-centric communications and continually test its effectiveness by running and monitoring such targeted online campaigns. The most prolific users, incidentally, are aged 16 to 24 (Ofcom 2012), and so online campaigns are likely to capture a younger audience overall than other more traditional practices.

In short, social media have already significantly altered how people make decisions about how they give their money and to whom they give it, and brands are now in the hands of the consumer. A new philosophy is required to truly see and be a part of the emerging big picture.

An inclusive viewpoint

Kate Nash is a passionate advocate for the empowerment of disabled people. While she was the chief executive of RADAR, in a personal interview in 2002, she suggested that her views concerning the disability movement are probably just as applicable to any minority grouping. Each form very important customer and supporter audiences as well as being the potential beneficiaries of the services of many CSOs. Thus marketeers must consider complex social needs. Nash pointed out, however, that in the case of disability, marketeers have not always done so, but that most disability charities worth their salt have now moved well away from sad images of disabled people who are in desperate need of the public's spare cash.

Equally, in the 2020s, marketing messages will need to be constructed for a distinctly different climate – a climate, at the very least, of changed economics, demography, public funding and delivery of services and society's expectations of what is socially (and medically) acceptable. The 1995 Disability Discrimination Act was designed to try to end discrimination against disabled people. While its remit was limited, and the powers of the Disability Rights Commission likewise, what it has done is to change the context within which disabled people are campaigning. The 2006 Equality Act merged the existing commissions and set up the Equality and Human Rights Commission in October 2007. As a result, the way in which disability organisations campaign and deliver services has had to change too. Gaining reasonable adjustments in the workplace is one thing. Tackling profound and deep-rooted assumptions about the value of life of disabled people continues to be quite another.

Once upon a time, in a different but far from dissimilar context, gay rights campaigner Tom Robinson sang: 'The buggers are legal now, what more are they after?' Marketeers, on behalf of disability organisations, will need to know the answer as well as find enticing ways of convincing a range of audiences that the need for change remains, the appetite for further work is acute and the achievability is real. The coming together of disability organisations with other similar interest groups may well be one very effective response to tackle that.

Service-dominant logic

For decades the marketing paradigm was built around the production and distribution of product. But, as noted in Chapter 1, Kotler and Levy (1969) broadened the concept of marketing in the 1970s and CSOs began to see the possibilities of using marketing practices to improve their competitive positioning. As customer relationship marketing (see page 12) gained ground over the 'traditional' transactional view of marketing, Burnett (1992) applied the principles of building relationships to fundraising. Because of this, CSOs gained confidence in making use of more aspects of the marketing mix. Moreover, Vargo and Lusch (2004) went so much further by defining service-dominant logic (SDL). This concept, in a nutshell, argues that you do not so much buy a car but interact with the company in the provision of a transport experience.

Dr John Egan (2011), marketing subject leader at London South Bank University, notes that at the heart of Vargo and Lusch's original concept there is a question. Whether, with so much fragmentation in marketing thought, the discipline was in fact moving towards a new, service-dominant logic which was, in turn, replacing the goods-dominant agenda which had ruled for most of the twentieth century. He goes on to state that:

> The service-centred view was, according to the authors, concerned with the identification and development of core competences and other entities (potential customers) that could benefit from these competences. Goods, it was determined, should no longer be seen as

the common denominator of exchange but rather the value lay in the application of specialist knowledge, mental skills and physical skills.

In other words, he is saying that goods are simply a physical representation of the organisation's skills and techniques and that, therefore, the purchase of a household item, for example, represents the acquisition of the skill, knowledge and other competences which go into manufacturing it in the first place. Egan paraphrases Vargo (2004), saying that 'value meanwhile, long recognised by marketers as the outcome of marketing effort, was reconceived as something created and determined by the user in the consumption process and only through use (so-called 'value-in-use') either directly or mediated by a good'. To put it simply, SDL-thinking says that an enterprise doesn't deliver value in the exchange but that the organisation only makes value propositions to the consumer who is actually the one who creates this value.

While certainly not without its critics, SDL has a mindset that is particularly useful for social marketeers who want to see those relationships with all the stakeholders not only brought to the fore but at the heart, philosophically, of the whole marketing strategy. Egan poses a somewhat rhetorical question about the possible long-term impact of SDL. 'Is service-dominant logic marketing's new paradigm or a passing fad? Time will tell. It does, in the meantime, however, offer marketers a new lens through which to examine our relationships with stakeholders.'

A call to action

Mark Astarita of the British Red Cross expressed in a personal interview in 2011 a rather different view of how things might develop for marketeers. He believes that the public face of most charities is, more often than not, carried through its fundraising messages. He stated that some will argue that this is as a direct consequence of the need to focus the potential giving audience on a call to action. Usually this action will be in the form of giving money and so there is a narrowing of the charity's brand down to a simple request for support. As the techniques which are employed by fundraisers are broadly similar in most charities and, for that matter, giver types are more often than not similar in terms of characteristics and demographics, the methods of communication end up looking similar. Finally, he noted that key messages will not differ overly whether money is raised for animals, young people, disabled people or overseas development.

So why should the principal vehicle by which people understand the brand values of a charity not be narrowed down to its sales proposition? Is it altogether a bad thing and is it likely to change much? It seems probable that fundraising expenditure is unlikely to diminish as a total proportion of charitable expenditure and may in fact increase in a competitive environment. Examine the annual report of any major charity and fundraising expenditure will almost always take second place ahead of everything except the primary purpose – charitable spend.

The vital importance of cause

Charities are one of the largest users of direct mail in the UK. Fundraisers are now beginning to turn their attention, some with great success, to direct-response television advertising. Many argue that charity brands need to operate more like the commercial sector. Why do you buy your Cola from Coca-Cola rather than from Virgin? Why not simply buy the supermarket own brand at a lower price?

Charities are *not* selling the same product, however; they are simply using the same techniques by which to make that sale. The NDCS (National Deaf Children's Society), for example, provides a variety of services for the nation's 35,000 deaf children and is very different in approach from the Action on Hearing Loss or the NSPCC, yet all three may well deploy the very same techniques in acquiring new givers or support.

It seems unlikely, therefore, that people buy brands in relation to charities. It is more certain that they buy causes and the way in which vision and mission are described for the cause will be the vital key to unlocking that support. However, it is probable that an understanding of SDL may help charities to develop and espouse the cause that much more effectively. For example, an umbrella training and education charity which normally offers a programme, or product range, of publications, training courses and conferences may begin to consider the whole journey that people entering the voluntary sector undertake (whether they are young graduates or chief executives, new volunteers or experienced campaigners and trustees).

Planned change

Planned giving

One of the changes that still may happen in the UK is the migration from the USA of 'planned giving'. It is reported that in the USA up to 40% of voluntary income derives from planned giving initiatives (Pybus 2002). The key difference between this and a conventional legacy bequest is that the gift is legally provided for in the lifetime of the giver and the recipient CSO has a financial interest in the gift (i.e. they can borrow against it as the gift is irrevocable). It does not, however, gain the full benefit until a deferred point, usually the death of the supporter. Financial products that allow planned giving to happen, and would be suitable for the UK market need to be designed, and financial services organisations will need to work very closely with charities to promote the benefits to prospective givers, whose knowledge and understanding of the tax implications lags way behind that of their US counterparts.

The previous government turned its face away from the idea of planned giving or even the tax-efficient charitable remainder trust, where assets or money are put into a trust (with an independent trustee) which cannot be withdrawn and will be given to charity on the death of the giver. The giver or other beneficiary receives income from it while living. However, with the coalition looking for good news that doesn't cost much, there may be opportunities. This is something that the European Association for Philanthropy and Giving has been campaigning about for years and Jim Myers, the organisation's founder and chair, remains ever optimistic. Sue Daniels, the current chief executive, feels that while the current government will do little in its first term, given a second, it may well implement change (personal communication 2011).

In memoriam giving

Very much in line with the concept of the Spectrum of Philanthropy discussed in Chapter 9 and potentially even more exciting than the Giving Campaign itself, may be the recent developments in the use of memorial or tribute funds which are aimed at involving supporters who make in memoriam donations.

In memoriam giving, whereby people make donations in memory of friends and loved ones, continues to be neglected, as shown by research conducted by Bluefrog (Ribeiro 2012). Charities generally have had few ideas about how to cultivate such support. In February 2003, however, not-for-profit marketing agency Whitewater attempted to change all that and to put in memoriam fundraising centre-stage. The agency developed successful strategies which began to change the way in which people give to charity. Unfortunately, however, it went into liquidation in 2012; but this did not spell the end of Whitewater's in memoriam fundraising website, Our Lasting Tribute. The site and its product offerings were acquired by charity direct marketing organisation, Valldata, a month after going into administration. In addition, there are now a number of fundraising sites and suppliers with tribute fund services and products.

The way that tribute funds work is by charities setting up funds which are named after the people who have passed away. Givers then have a vehicle through which to donate and raise money, forever, in the name of the person whom they have lost. This strategy aims to bring charitable giving closer to people's hearts, and to inspire people to give and raise more. It could bring people into the world of charity giving who have not responded to other appeals to date. What is more, it could bring a new generation of younger supporters to various causes. Younger people tend to ignore direct mail, but will they ignore text messages or emails from a relative or family member about the fund named after 'grandma'? An ask for a gift in memory of a loved one, parent, partner or child is possibly the most powerful ask of all.

Whitewater passionately believed that these totally unrestricted funds will generate long-term income streams and ultimately significantly increase legacy income. In a personal interview in 2007 former chair Steve Andrews said, 'The possibilities are endless... This is an approach with the capacity to increase the numbers of in memoriam donors and then dramatically increase their lifetime values. It's giving donors what they want!'

The next decade may see rather more movement in this area and potentially change the face of relationship fundraising forever. Even where charities have not adopted proactive strategies to promote these named funds, a revised, more appropriate, approach to in memoriam donations could increase the numbers and values very significantly. The potential can be summed up in a personal anecdote about the author's mother.

Peggy Maple died leaving a modest legacy to her six favourite causes. Six cheques were despatched and five thank you letters received, with no follow-up from any of them. However, the fundraiser at the sixth, a small charity called the Friends of Pershore Abbey rang with an effusive thank you and an unbeatable proposition. 'Lovely woman your mother, I was very fond of her. You probably didn't know that she was paying to have the floodlights on in the abbey in memory of your father, your brother and your grandmother. You'll probably want to cancel them, won't you?' Of course, not only were they renewed but a fourth evening's subscription was paid for in her memory. What is even more important is that, in the fullness of time, the Friends of Pershore Abbey which hitherto was certainly not one of the author's favourite causes will find its way into his will. Giving in memory of a loved one is probably the most powerful single motivator that there is. Thus a suitable, relevant, tribute device is, as a marketing communication, second to none.

The Funding Commission

NCVO set up the Funding Commission in 2009 to look into the future of charity funding. In a personal interview in 2011 Richard Gutch, Secretary to the Commission, said that 'the timing of the Commission's work has been challenging. The decade of growth for charities (from £25 billion to £35 billion), fuelled by public sector contracts, individual giving and trading is over.' He went on to ask whether we are on the edge of a precipice or whether, with the right measures, the sector could continue to grow stronger.

The Commission presented its report, *Funding the Future*, along with some specific recommendations in the summer of 2011. The report states that there are five developments, which will have a particular influence on the future funding of CSOs:

1.   an ageing population;

2.   a more diverse population and household structure;

3.   development of new technology;

4.   climate change;

5.   ethical consumerism and social values.

The report goes on to say that these long-term changes are taking place independently of the government, although, clearly, government policies can affect the impact that they have. Other more immediate changes are the result of action by the government itself and, again, five stand out:

1.   public finance deficit reduction;

2.   the Big Society initiative;

3.   localism;

4.   reform of public services;

5.   transparency and accountability.

Funding Commission 2010

The report presents two scenarios for the future. Under one, public services will be cut severely, thereby serving fewer and fewer people. Many of the services that are left will be taken over and run by commercial organisations which will work within narrow eligibility criteria under large-scale, performance-based contracts. The public sector will protect its own and CSOs become desperately overstretched and unsustainable through funding reductions, owing to an unrealistic assumption that government support can be replaced by voluntary effort and income. The cuts in public services and welfare benefits mean that disadvantaged communities will suffer most and inequalities will increase.

Under the alternative scenario, it envisages, instead of a steady decline, a fundamental shift where public services and models for delivery will be altered using innovative partnerships between the public, for-profit and not-for-profit sectors. This 'new social contract' will involve new financing arrangements that would increase voluntary income. Government investment and commercial sponsorship help CSOs to realise their full potential and local people and service users become central in helping to determine the future.

The Commission was particularly concerned that, despite the government's rhetoric on the Big Society initiative, there is a real danger that the first scenario will become a reality. Nevertheless, the Commission agreed that certain areas of income may increase in real terms by 2020 – individual giving from £11.3 billion to £20 billion; trading income by £1.8 billion; and grants from companies by perhaps nearly £1 billion – and that the share and quality of public sector contracts delivered by CSOs could also rise. The *Funding the Future* report also states that the Commission believes new approaches to social investment can attract £10 billion more private investment and that consequently the sector can become 'better capitalised and more resilient' (Funding Commission 2010).

However, in order for this second scenario to become a reality and to have a profound impact upon the sector, the Commission's recommendations will have to be adopted and so the scope of the following four main recommendations is considered in the report more fully.

Firstly, CSOs will have to 'step up to the mark' by getting better at measuring, reporting and increasing impact; increasing financial capability; making better use of social media and technology; promoting their value to commissioners; working collaboratively; and developing infrastructure that is sustainable and effective. It states that the way infrastructure is currently structured is unsustainable and, in some instances, incomplete. It recommends formalised collaborative working as necessary, including a coordinated programme of mergers.

Secondly, funders and commissioners must use current resources better in order to help CSOs increase impact and financial capability. Funding strategies must take account of changes in the wider funding environment, which may impact on unpopular causes or disadvantaged groups in particular. Trusts and foundations could consider, for example, investing more of their assets to promote their charitable objects.

Thirdly, NCVO will have to work very hard with other infrastructure bodies to increase the sector's income. With an ageing population, the impending retirement of baby boomers (the wealthiest generation there has ever been – see Chapter 9, page 132) and an increase in the very rich, individual giving can increase significantly over the next ten years. For that to happen, however, everyone involved, especially trustees, needs to get far better at asking people to give and at engaging those who do. With better access to capital, markets and skills, trading income can rise, as can commercial giving, through better engagement with companies, locally as well as nationally.

Lastly, and importantly, the Commission states that the government must play its part. While it may not be the time to make lots of new demands, government resources are needed to help fund collaborative working and a series of targeted small-grant programmes for Big Society initiatives. There also needs to be a radical redesign of commissioning, which allows users to determine what services are needed and how they are best delivered, rather than simply continuing with current public service models on reduced budgets. One thing that the government could ensure is that the Big Society Bank plays a key strategic role in attracting private capital into the sector through developing new financial mechanisms and underwriting investor risk.

Consultations on sector infrastructure, the follow-on from the *Giving White Paper* and ongoing debate about the government's Big Society initiative all provide plenty of opportunities for ensuring that the Commission's recommendations are read, understood and have the chance of making a real impact.

However, in an environment where the retreat of government is causing rising inequality in income and wealth distribution, it is worth mentioning, as a footnote, some of the key observations from *The Spirit Level* (Wilkinson and Pickett 2009). Put simply, in developed-world countries where disparities of wealth are least (such as Denmark, Sweden, Finland and Holland) there are much lower levels of social need and mental and physical health issues, and much higher levels of societal trust and well-being when compared with countries (such as the USA, Portugal and the UK) where disparities of wealth are greatest. This is a sobering thought for CSOs that are striving to address some of those societal needs.

Mixed joint campaigns

As discussed in chapters 7 and 8, charities generally have distinct advantages when it comes to developing and delivering communications strategies. Strong, urgent, powerful messages can be constructed and delivered whatever the medium chosen. Increasingly, it will be the norm to use multimedia. The use of multimedia provides a huge opportunity for commercial marketeers to apply some of their far more substantial promotional budgets creatively, providing innovative solutions and propositions for customers and supporters alike. An excellent example is that of the Triodos Bank piggybacking on the well-recognised ethical reputations of Amnesty International and Oxfam to reinforce its own ethical philosophy and practices. A much greater use of mixed joint campaigns will surely follow.

The ability of CSOs to reach fragmented but highly motivated audiences will be crucial in all of this. Their understanding and use of the changing channels of communication will be a major factor in determining who succeeds and who is left behind. As Kim Roberts of London South Bank University commented in a personal interview in 2012, it would be folly for charities to ignore the possibilities of working more intelligently, across the usual divides, to reach audiences more effectively.

As has been discussed, in the UK (unlike in the USA) the richest give the least in percentage terms. That is, those earning under £32,000 per annum give more than 1% of their income while those earning more than £52,000 a year give less than 0.8% of their income. One of the Giving Campaign's objectives that was set out in 2004 is the aspiration of persuading givers to increase donations to around 1.5% of income. In 2011, John Low, Chief Executive of CAF, called for a continuance of this aspiration with a particular emphasis upon the wealthiest in society (Hudson 2011). As 85% of the 2010 Sunday Times Rich List have made their wealth rather than inherited it (Beresford 2010), it is reasonable to conclude that the majority of the wealthiest in society today are working for or running successful companies. This increase in giving among the baby boomers and Jonesers is then perhaps the aspiration, or even the vision, that giving consortia could get behind and work towards achieving in the next decade.

Conclusion

In reality, of course, only time will tell what the marketing challenges will be. Most certainly the world may change a lot less than we think. Tim Berners-Lee (a former president of the RSA and one of the World Wide Web pioneers) is widely quoted on the Web as saying in July 1997 that 'If we know what the future is we aren't looking far enough ahead.'

In 1995, a number of contributors to the publication *From Mailshots to the Millennium* tried to look ahead and make predictions about what might be happening in five to ten years' time: John Rodd, for example, postulated that in the year 2000 Abel Newman, a fundraising director, could well be using video conferencing, 'talking to' his computer and using 'logic manager' to plan communications and fast track potential high-value givers. All the technology required for this vision is available today but how effectively are fundraisers using it? More pragmatically, elsewhere in the same publication contributors John Rawlinson and Joe Saxton commented:

> Too many charity marketers still believe their business is fundraising. We believe this is an outdated view – that business is actually to create visions of a better world and to persuade people to support that vision by donating. It is about giving people the opportunity to make statements on who they are and what they believe in. It is about building the kind of relationship with them that enables them to further their dreams and feel good about it.
>
> Maple et al. 1995

Rawlinson and Saxton went on to describe charity marketing as being in the 'Model T age' (i.e. stuck between 1909 and 1927). Perhaps by now it's more equivalent to a Ford Escort but it still lags behind strong commercial models which are now well into hybrids. The challenge of the next decade will be to catch up and overtake the commercial models of today. Organisations, both for-profit and not-for-profit, which integrate fully, plan and remain open to opportunities, will succeed. Flexibility within well-considered and effective strategies that are in accord with meaningful visions and missions will enable those which are best able to 'seize the day'.

The clearest conclusion is that CSOs and commercial organisations can work far more closely, creatively and in a mutually beneficial way. Even the august CIM endorses this approach in 'Shape the Agenda' (CIM 2009b). The report agrees with the contentions argued here in the first edition, that the commercial sector has much to learn from social marketing and much to gain by greater cooperation. The launch in January 2013 of Collaborate – a community interest company that will promote more effective collaboration between the public, business and social sectors and is a partnership between London South Bank University, Serco, Calouste Gulbenkian Foundation and the National Housing Federation – may be just such a manifestation (Youde 2013).

There is, then, the potential for great profit and life enhancement in this route towards collaboration, but it requires movement from all sides to make it a reality. This surely is an unbeatable proposition.

References

Alleyne, Richard (2002), 'Imperial and UCL discuss merger to be world player', *The Telegraph*, 15 October

Allford, Marion (1993), *Charity Appeals*, London, JM Dent & Sons

Alter, Kim (n.d.), 'Social Enterprise Typology' [web paper], www.4lenses.org/setypology, Virtue Ventures, accessed 7 January 2013

Ansoff, H. Igor (1968), *Corporate Strategy*, London, Penguin

ARM (2003), *ARM Annual Report and Accounts 2003*, Cambridge, ARM Holdings

ASA (2008), 'World Villages for Children' [within a log of online database cases], www.asa.org.uk, Advertising Standards Authority, case dated 16 July 2008

Assisi (2011), *The Assisi Animal Charities Foundation Charity (A Company Limited by Guarantee) Commission Copy Annual Report and Accounts for the Year Ended 31 December 2010*, www.charitycommission.gov.uk, dated 2011, accessed 15 November 2012

Assisi (2012), *The Assisi Animal Charities Foundation (A Company Limited by Guarantee) Charity Commission Copy Annual Report and Accounts for the Year Ended 31 December 2011*, www.charitycommission.gov.uk, dated 2012, accessed 15 November 2012

Attwood, Karen (2008), 'Pret a Manger chain sold to private equity firm Bridgepoint in £350m deal', *The Independent*, 23 February

Barnardo's (2012), 'Advertising campaigns' [web page], www.barnardos.org.uk, dated 2012, accessed 21 November 2012

Batten, L. (2002), 'Market Research Budgets' [specially commissioned report on the spending of leading charities], London, Crossbow Research, May

BBC (2009), 'VAT abolished on text donations' [online article], news.bbc.co.uk, dated 26 July 2009, accessed 17 December 2012

Beckett, Francis, (2010), *What Did the Baby Boomers Ever Do For Us?*, London, Biteback Publishing

Beresford, P. (2010), *Sunday Times Rich List*, London, A & C Black

BIS (2011), *A Guide to Legal Forms for Social Enterprise*, London, Department for Business, Innovation and Skills, Crown Copyright

BITC (2003), *The Business Case for Corporate Responsibility*, London, Business in the Community

BITC (2010), *The Business Case for Being a Responsible Business*, London, Business in the Community

Branchu, Florence (2011), *If the Baby-boomers are acting philanthropically differently from previous generations, then how will this change in behaviour translate into legacy gifts? A study of changing behaviour towards charitable gifts in wills*, dissertation for MSc Charity Marketing and Fundraising, London South Bank University

The Brooke (2012), *The Brooke Hospital for Animals Annual Report and Account for the Year Ended 31 March 2012*, London, The Brooke

Bruce, Ian (2005), *Charity Marketing: Meeting Need Through Customer Focus*, London, ICSA Publishing

Burnett, Ken (1992), *Relationship Fundraising*, London, White Lion Press

Burnett, Ken (1996a), 'The Future of Relationship Fundraising: What's Next' [online PDF], www.tgci.com, The Grantsmanship Center, dated 1996, accessed 1 November 2012

Burnett, Ken (1996b), *Friends for Life: Relationship Fundraising in Practice*, London, White Lion Press

Business In the Environment (2001), *Investing in the Future, City Attitudes to Environmental and Social Issues*, London, Business in the Community

Cabinet Office (2012*), Trusted and Independent: Giving charity back to charities; Review of the Charities Act 2006*, presented to Parliament by the Minister for the Cabinet Office, pursuant to section 73 of the Charities Act 2006, London, The Stationery Office

CAF (2002), Charities Aid Foundation Annual Conference and Exhibition: 'Does Charity Matter?', London, 7 November

CAF & NCVO (2010), *UK Giving 2010 Trends and Characteristics*, London, Charities Aid Foundation and National Council for Voluntary Organisations

Carlson, Martin E. (1968), *Why People Give*, New York, Council Press for Stewardship and Benevolence

Charity Commission (2010), 'World Villages for Children: Summary Information Return 2009 (Online)' [web document], www.charitycommission.gov.uk, document dated 27 October 2010, accessed 14 September 2011

Charity Commission (2011), '1058973 – World Villages For Children' [web page – charity overview], www.charitycommission.gov.uk, dated 2011, accessed 14 September 2011

Charity Commission (2012), 'More than just a Number: Themes and trends in charity registrations (Issue 2)' [online PDF], www.charitycommission.gov.uk, dated 2012, accessed 14 November 2012

CIM (2009a), *Marketing and the 7Ps: A Brief Summary of Marketing and How it Works*, Maidenhead, Chartered Institute of Marketing

CIM (2009b), 'Shape the Agenda', *The Marketer*, issue 15, pp. 46–49

CIM (2012), 'History' [web page], www.cim.co.uk/About/History.aspx, Chartered Institute of Marketing, dated 2012, accessed 1 November 2012

CIMA (2011), 'The world's corporate reporting system is at risk' [online press release], www.cimaglobal.com, dated May 2011

Clark, Jenny, David Kane, Karl Wilding, Peter Bass (2012), *The UK Civil Society Almanac 2012*, London, NCVO

Clark, Nicola (2008), 'McDonald's tops hated brands poll, while Beckham and Katona most loathed celebs', *Marketing*, 13 May

Clausewitz, General Carl von (1874), *On War*, translated by Colonel J.J. Graham

Colenso BBDO (2010), 'Ignore' [print advertisement], Auckland, New Zealand, Colenso BBDO advertising agency

Cooperative Bank (2003), 'Campaign Analysis: Cluster Bombs' [web page], www.co-operativebank.co.uk [web page], dated March 2003, accessed 10 October 2011

Cope, Nigel (2002), 'Tax break saves entrepreneurs £440,000', *The Independent*, October 25

Cracknell, Richard (2010), 'The ageing population: The UK's ageing population has considerable consequences for public services' [online document], www.parliament.uk, House of Commons Library Research, dated 2010, accessed 31 October 2011

Cram, Tony (2001), *Customers that Count: How to Build Living Relationships With Your Most Valuable Customers*, London, Financial Times Prentice Hall

Dawkins, Richard (1976), *The Selfish Gene*, Oxford University Press

Department for Communities and Local Government (2011), *Citizenship Survey: 2010–11 (April 2010 – March 2011), England*, Crown Copyright

DMIS (2005), Direct Mail Response Rates Survey, Direct Mail Information Service, published March 2005

Dobbs, Joy, Véronique Jochum, Karl Wilding, Liz Lipscomb, Malcolm Smith and Richard Harrison (2011), *UK Giving 2011: An overview of charitable giving in the UK, 2010/11*, London and West Malling, NCVO and CAF

Dobbs, Joy, Véronique Jochum, Karl Wilding, Malcolm Smith, Richard Harrison (2012), *UK Giving 2012: An overview of charitable giving in the UK, 2011/12*, London and West Malling, NCVO and CAF

DPWMF (2000), *The Work Continues: Annual Review 2000*, London, The Diana, Princess of Wales Memorial Fund

DPWMF (2012), 'Fund awards legacy grants and releases details about its planned closure in December' [online press release], www.theworkcontinues.org, The Diana, Princess of Wales Memorial Fund, dated 27 November

Drummond, Graeme and John Ensor (2001), *Strategic Marketing*, Oxford, Butterworth Heinemann

DWP (2011), 'Disability prevalence estimates 2010/11' [online PDF], odi.dwp.gov.uk, dated 2011, accessed 12 December 2012

Edge, Laura Bufano (2003), *Andrew Carnegie: Industrial Philanthropist*, Minneapolis MN, Lerner Publishing

Egan, John (2011), *Relationship Marketing: Exploring Relational Strategies in Marketing*, Harlow, Pearson Education

England Hockey (2012), 'Hockey receives participation boost' [online press release] www.englandhockey.co.uk, dated 22 June 2012, accessed 13 November 2012

Fishbein, Martin and Icek Ajzen (1975), *Belief, Attitude, Intention, and Behavior: An Introduction to Theory and Research*, Reading MA, Addison-Wesley

French, Alan (2006), *The Guide to UK Company Giving*, London, Directory of Social Change

FRSB (2011), *Confident About Fundraising – Annual Report 2010/2011*, London, Fundraising Standards Board

FRSB (2012), *Good Honest Fundraising – Annual Report 2012*, London, Fundraising Standards Board

Funding Commission (2010), *Funding the Future: A 10-year Framework for Civil Society*, London, NCVO

Gaines, Sara (2002), 'Joining forces boosts impact', *The Guardian*, 25 September

GCA (2012), 'Facts and Figures' [web page], www.greetingcardassociation.org.uk, The Greeting Card Association, dated 2012, accessed 1 November 2012

The Goldonian (2010), 'Dr Thomas Barnardo' [web page], www.goldonian.org/barnardo/drbarnardo.htm, dated 8 December 2010

Gray, Robert (2003), 'Direct Mail: Green Letter Days', *Third Sector*, 8 October

Green, Brian (2002), 'A question of ethics', *Construction News*, 17 October

Gutch, Richard (2012), *The Good Mergers Guide*, London, Prospectus & Eastside

Hewson, A. (1997), Address to the trustees of Arthritis Care, Annual General Meeting held in October 1997, Arthritis Care

Hill, Nicola (2002), 'Minister on a mission', *Society Guardian*, 2 October

Howard, James (2012), 'Rising demand for investments capable of doing well, as well as doing good', www.financialreporter.co.uk, dated 12 November

Hudson, Sophie (2011), 'People earning less than £32k give higher proportion of their income than others', Third Sector Online, 3 November

IBFAN (2012), 'Overview of the Nestlé Boycott' [web page], www.ibfan.org, International Baby Food Action Network, dated 2012, accessed 21 November 2012

Imperial College London (2012), 'Cystic fibrosis gene therapy programme gets green light with public funding' [online press release], www3.imperial.ac.uk, dated 16 March 2012, accessed 1 December 2012

Islamic Relief (2012), 'About us' [web page], www.islamic-relief.org.uk, dated 2012, accessed 12 December 2012

Kane, David and James Allen (2011), *Counting the Cuts: The Impact of Spending Cuts on the UK Voluntary and Community Sector*, NCVO

Kay-Williams, Susan (2000), 'The five stages of fundraising: a framework for the development of fundraising', *International Journal of Nonprofit and Voluntary Sector Marketing*, vol. 5, no. 3, pp. 220–240

Kotler, Philip (1975), *Marketing for Nonprofit Organizations*, Englewood Cliffs NJ, Prentice-Hall

Kotler, Philip (1994), *Marketing Management: Analysis, Planning, Implementation, and Control*, Englewood Cliffs NJ, Prentice-Hall

Kotler, Philip (1999), *Kotler on Marketing*, New York, The Free Press (Simon & Schuster)

Kotler, Philip and Levy, Sidney (1969), 'A New form of Marketing Myopia: Rejoinder to professor luck', *AMA Journal of Marketing*, vol. 33, issue 3, pp. 55–57

Lake, Howard (2009), 'The Story so far: Charity Websites and Email' [slide presentation], presented at the Internet Fundraising and Social Media Conference, Institute of Fundraising South West, Bristol, 16 June

LCD (2012), *Annual Report and Accounts – 2011/12*, London, Leonard Cheshire Disability

Legacy Foresight (2012), *Legacy Market Snapshot: Summary Report 2012*, Legacy Monitor Consortium, supported by Remember A Charity

Lillya, Denise (2011), *The Guide to UK Company Giving*, London, Directory of Social Change

Lloyd, Bruce and Susan Clayton (2002), 'Planning for the Future', *Professional Manager*, vol. 11, issue 4, pp. 32–33

Lloyd, Theresa, (2004), *Why Rich People Give*, London, Association of Charitable Foundations

Lombard, Daniel (2012), 'Tesco charity of the year partnership with Alzheimer's charities raises £7.5m', *Third Sector*, 27 April

Low, Natalie, Sarah Butt, Angela Ellis Paine and Justin Davis Smith (2007), *Helping Out: A national survey of volunteering and charitable giving*, London, Cabinet Office

MacLeod, Donald (2002), 'Opposition ends Imperial and UCL merger', *The Guardian*, 18 November

Maple, Peter, Joe Saxton, Chris Carnie, Jon Rodd, Angela Heylin, Ian Bruce and John Rawlinson (1995), *From Mailshots to the Millennium*, London, Third Sector

Maple, Peter (2008), 'The Spectrum of Philanthropy', *Caritis – Not for Profit Journal*, May, pp. 38–44

Maple, Peter, (2009), 'How UK Charities Treat Major Donors', Dissemination Seminar, London, London South Bank University, July

Maple, Peter (2011), 'Fundraising Outlook', presentation at IOF Consultants Group, May

McKie, Robin, (2006), 'Charities Step in to help Cystic Fibrosis Sufferers', *The Observer*, 3 December

Merriam Webster (2012), online word search, www.merriamwebster.com, accessed 12 December 2012

Mitchell, Colin (2002), 'Selling the brand inside' *Harvard Business Review*, January

Mitie (2012), '25th Anniversary – Celebrating 25 years of success!', www.mitie.com, dated 2012, accessed 26 November 2012

Morris, Richard (2000), *Cheshire: The Biography of Leonard Cheshire, VC, OM*, London, Viking Press

Mullin, Redmond (2002), *Fundraising Strategy*, London, Directory of Social Change

Murdock, Alex (2010), 'Social Enterprise' in the *International Encyclopedia of Civil Society, Volume 3*, Helmut K. Anheier and Stefan Toepler (eds), Springer Science and Business Media, pp. 1410–1414

Muspratt, Caroline (2006), 'Fink gives £4m to charity' [online article], www.telegraph.co.uk, dated 17 November

NCVO (2007), *Faith and voluntary action: an overview of current evidence and debates*, London, National Council for Voluntary Organisations

nfpSynergy (n.d.), 'Charity Awareness Monitor Briefing Pack' [online PDF], nfpsynergy.net, accessed 5 December 2012

nfpSynergy (2010), 'Charity Awareness Monitor' [awareness tracking service], London, nfpSynergy

Nyssens, M. (2006), *Social Enterprise – At the Crossroads of Market, Public Policies and Civil Society*, London and New York, Routledge

Ofcom (2012), 'Adults media use and attitudes report 2012' [online research document], stakeholders.ofcom.org.uk, dated May 2012

O'Hara, Mary (2002), 'Faith, Hope and a Job with a Charity', *The Guardian*, 14 September

Oliver, Mark and Zeta McDonald (2002), 'The echoes of Barnardo's altered imagery', *The Guardian*, 3 October

OUP (2009), Oxford Dictionary of Quotations, Oxford University Press

PFRA (2012), 'Why do charities use F2F fundraising?' [web page], www.pfra.org.uk/face-to-face_fundraising, dated 2012, accessed 15 November 2012

Pharoah, Cathy (2008), 'Across the pond' [web article], www.charitiesdirect.com/caritas-magazine, dated 2008, accessed 8 November 2012

Pharoah, Cathy (2010), 'Charity Income Trends' [PowerPoint presentation], Cass Business School and Centre for Charitable Giving and Philanthropy (CGAP), presented at IOF Consultants Special Interest Group, February

Prasad, Raekha (2002), 'Branded for life: Samaritans' new image to reflect its wide-ranging role', *The Guardian*, 2 October

Prince, Russ Alan and Karen Maru File (1994), *The Seven Faces of Philanthropy: A New Approach to Cultivating Major Donors*, New York, Jossey-Bass

Pontell, Jonathan (2005), 'The Jones Generation' [web page], www.jonathanpontell.com, dated 2005, accessed 18 October 2011

Pybus, Julie (2002), 'Will planned giving work in the UK?', *Third Sector*, 17 April

Quelch, John A., Nathalie Laidler-Kylander (2006), *The New Global Brands*, Mason OH, South-Western College

Rangan, V. Kasturi, Herman B. Leonard and Susan McDonald (2008), 'The Future of Social Enterprise Harvard Business School Working Paper', www.hbs.edu, dated June 2008, accessed 28th October 2011

Remember A Charity (2011), *Impact Report 2011*, www.rememberacharity.org.uk, dated 2011, accessed 31 October 2012

Ribeiro, Celina (2012), 'Charities are missing a trick on in-memoriam giving', *Civil Society*, 13 November

Ridley-Duff, Rory and Mike Bull (2011), *Understanding Social Enterprise: Theory and Practice*, London, Sage Publications

Ries, Al and Jack Trout (1989), *Bottom-Up Marketing*, New York, McGraw-Hill

Roberts, Kim and Beverley Barker (2010), 'Consumer Centric Marketing Communications Models: Does web 2.0 demand a new one?', Academy of Marketing Conference 2010, Academy of Marketing, Coventry

Rodgers, F. G. (1986), *The IBM Way*, London, Guild Publishing

Sargeant, Adrian and Jen Shang (2009), 'Clear Insights: Philanthropic Psychology', *Advancing Philanthropy*, June, pp. 29–33

Saxton, Joe (2002) *Polishing the Diamond*, London, nfpSynergy

Saxton, Joe (2010), from restricted Future Foundation figures and used in a number of his presentations in 2010

Schindler, Robert M. (1992), 'The Real Lesson of New Coke: the Value of Focus Groups for Predicting the Effects of Social Influence', *Marketing Research*, December

Scope (2001), 'The Spastics Society to Scope: The story of the name change and relaunch November 1994' [online PDF], www.scope.org.uk, dated 2001, accessed 5 December 2012

Searight, Sarah (1993), *Oasis: 60 years of the Brooke Hospital for Animals*, London, Brooke Hospital for Animals

Shelter (2004), *Shelter Report and Accounts 2003–04*, London, Shelter

SOFII (2010), 'Paul the apostle motivates his church's donors – c. 56 AD' [web page], www.sofii.org/node/499, dated 2012, accessed 29 November 2012

Stern, Carl W. and George Stalk (1998), *Perspectives on Strategy: From the Boston Consulting Group*, Chichester, John Wiley & Sons

Stothart, Chloe (2012), 'The religious give more to charity, according to CAF report', www.thirdsector.co.uk, Third Sector Online, dated 23 February, accessed 15 November 2012

Strauss, William and Neil Howe (1991), *Generations: The History of America's Future from 1584 to 2069*, New York, Quill

Stroud, Lawrence (1995), National Fundraising Convention workshop, Birmingham

The Telegraph (2000), 'Lady Ryder of Warsaw', The Telegraph Media Group, 3 November

Third Sector (2007), 'Hot issue: Will charities continue to use overseas challenge events?' [online article], www.thirdsector.co.uk, dated 9 May 2007, accessed 15 January 2013

Third Sector Research (2009, 2012), 'Charity Brand Index' [survey], Third Sector Research, in association with PRWeek and Harris Interactive

Thirkettle, G.L. (1970), *Basic Economics*, London, Macdonald & Evans

Titmuss, Richard (1972), *The Gift Relationship: from Human Blood to Social Policy*, London, Vintage Books

Tocqueville, Alexis de (1998), *Democracy in America*, Ware, Wordsworth Editions, pp. 229–236

Tracey, Gemma, Jon Matthews and Joe Saxton (2011), *Passion, Persistence, and Partnership: the Secrets of Earning More Online*, nfpSynergy, MissionFish and the Institute of Fundraising

Turner, Howard (2012), '10.2 Costs of tax relief' [table 10.2], www.hmrc.gov.uk, HM Revenue and Customs

Vargo, Stephen L. and Robert F. Lusch (2004), 'Evolving to a New Dominant Logic for Marketing', *Journal of Marketing*, vol. 68, no.1, pp. 1–17

Wiggins, Kaye (2011), 'Labour conference debates give pointers to future policy', *Third Sector*, 4 October

Wilkinson, Richard and Kate Pickett (2009), *The Spirit Level*, London, Penguin

WWE (2002), 'World Wrestling Federation Entertainment drops the 'F'!' [online press release], corporate.wwe.com, dated 6 May, accessed 30 November 2012

Youde, Kate (2013), 'Community interest company Collaborate outlines its intentions', www.thirdsector.co.uk, Third Sector Online, dated 17 January

All epigraphs are widely quoted on the Internet, except for:

Bruce, Ian (2005), *Charity Marketing: Meeting Need Through Customer Focus*, London, ICSA Publishing

Karass, C. (1970), *The Negotiating Game*, New York, Thomas Y Crowell

McLaren, Malcolm (1998), interview for *Muse* magazine, September

Further reading

Baguley John (2000), *Successful Fundraising*, Stafford, Bibliotek Books, 2nd edn

Becker, G.S. (1976), 'Altruism, egoism, and genetic fitness', *Journal of Economic Literature*, vol. 4, no. 3, pp. 817–826

Handy, Charles and Elizabeth Handy (2006), *The New Philanthropists*, London, Random House

Kotler, Philip and Nancy R. Lee (2008), *Social Marketing – Influencing Behaviours for Good*, London, Sage Publications, 3rd edn

Sargeant, Adrian (2009), *Marketing Management for Nonprofit Organisations*, Oxford University Press, 3rd edn

Stapleton, J. (1975), *Marketing*, Sevenoaks, Hodder & Stoughton

Ven, Jeroen van de (2000), 'The Economics of the Gift', Discussion Paper 2000–68, Tilburg University, Center for Economic Research

Wallace, Danny (2004), *Random Acts of Kindness*, London, Random House

Willmott, Michael (2001), *Citizen Brands*, Chichester, John Wiley & Sons

Index